BOEING

BOEING

From Peashooter to Jumbo

DAVID LEE

CHARTWELL
BOOKS, INC.

A QUINTET BOOK

Published by Chartwell Books
A Division of Book Sales, Inc.
114 Northfield Avenue
Edison, New Jersey 08337

ISBN 0-7858-1044-7

This book was designed and produced by
Quintet Publishing Limited
6 Blundell Street
London N7 9BH

Creative Director: Richard Dewing
Designer: Ian Hunt
Senior Editor: Clare Hubbard
Editor: Andrew Armitage

Typeset in Great Britain by
Central Southern Typesetters, Eastbourne
Manufactured in Hong Kong by Regent Publishing Services Ltd
Printed in Singapore by Star Standard Industries (Pte) Ltd

CONTENTS

INTRODUCTION

Boeing—it's a name that has conjured up many different associations over the past 90 years. Toward the end of the first decade of the twentieth century and into the second, to the residents of Seattle, Boeing meant lumber and boats. By the end of the second decade, when aviation had begun to make its mark, the name Boeing meant a Pacific Coast constructor of seaplanes for the US Navy. From the mid-1920s for more than a decade the name became synonymous with fighters culminating in the famous "Peashooter." Many in this period also associated Boeing with the carrying of mail and passengers.

By the end of the fourth decade Boeing meant Big Bombers, a connotation it retains to this day, with its legendary B-52 Stratofortress. As the twentieth century moved into its second half, Boeing became *the* name for jet airliners. The 707 introduced continental and intercontinental jet travel. The resulting demand for jets at the smaller airports was met by the 727 and later by the 737. The incredible 747, the first and only true "jumbo jet" shrank the world, bringing international travel within the reach of all. The 757, 767, and 777 have all built on the irresistible impression that all the world flies on a Boeing.

This book will attempt to illustrate the story of the Boeing airplane from its tiny beginnings in 1916 to today, when the Boeing Company is the largest aerospace company in the world. At the end of 1997, Boeing and its subsidiaries employed over

BELOW Based at Phoenix, Arizona, America West Airlines operates a mixed fleet of Airbus and Boeing designs, including 14 Boeing 757s on routes throughout the USA.

237,000 people worldwide and earned nearly 46 billion dollars. Its products are not only civil and military aircraft but also missiles, commercial space technology (including satellites, space craft, and rockets), electronics and computers, and their applications. In the past, the Boeing Company has built lunar orbiters, lunar roving vehicles, hydrofoils, and aero engines. In financially desperate times, the company has diversified into furniture making, desalination plants, speedboats, railcars, and even farming.

To do justice to the whole story would take a library of books. Therefore, this book limits its scope to an examination of Boeing aircraft. Also, in the long history of a company that mirrors the history of aviation itself, only those aircraft that are generally considered to have been successful or to have had technological significance are covered.

This history is being written at a time of great change within the Boeing Company. Boeing has acquired other companies throughout its history but the acquisitions of 1996 and 1997

overshadow all others. A full history of Boeing aircraft could embrace not only the Stearman trainers and Vertol helicopters (which are included) but also the complete Douglas line dating back to 1921; the North American fighters and bombers from the incredible P-51 Mustang onward; McDonnell jet fighters, including the incomparable F4 Phantom II; and helicopters from Hughes! We're back to needing a whole library of books! Therefore, with just an occasional exception, Douglas, North American, McDonnell, and Hughes are not part of this story.

ABOVE Photographed in 1988, Boeing's Minuteman Intercontinental Ballistic Missile (ICBM) stands guard in front of the Headquarters of the Strategic Air Command at Offutt Air Force Base, Nebraska.

RIGHT Displayed on the left in the Missile Park at the superb USAF Museum, Wright-Patterson Air Force Base, Ohio, is Boeing's first missile, the IM-99 Bomarc. With a range of over 400 miles, the supersonic Bomarc was designed in the mid-1950s to intercept enemy bombers.

CHAPTER ONE

THE BOEING COMPANY

LEFT To commemorate its 50th anniversary in 1966, Boeing built and flew this replica (Model 1A) of their first aircraft, the B&W.

ABOVE A contemporary view of the single float version of the Model 5, the C-1F, moored in 1918 on the slipway of the hangar on Lake Union, Seattle.

GENESIS

In the beginning was the purchase of the Heath shipyard on the Duwamish River in Seattle, Washington, by William Boeing in March 1910. This was to be his first aircraft factory and later Plant One. Also in that year, he attended America's first airplane meeting in Los Angeles, returning fired with enthusiasm for the new technology.

One of his fellow enthusiasts at Seattle's University Club was Conrad Westervelt, a navy engineer with aeronautical qualifications from the renowned Massachusetts Institute of Technology. Both read, studied, and discussed how they might become involved in aviation. Finally in July 1915 Boeing had his first aircraft flight, which convinced him that he should learn to fly.

He took lessons from one of America's great aviation pioneers, Glenn Martin, from whom he also bought a Martin seaplane. Around this time Boeing and Westervelt agreed to design and build their own aircraft. With parts, including the floats, being made at the Heath shipyard, assembly of their first aircraft began in the new hangar that had been erected beside Lake Union to house the Martin seaplane.

THE B&W (later Model 1)

Named after the initials of its designers, Boeing's first airplane, christened Bluebill, made its maiden flight on June 15, 1916 with William Boeing at the controls. Westervelt was not there to see it. Despite his protests, the navy had posted him back East and he was to play no further part in the Boeing story.

To market the B&W (a second was built), Boeing established the Pacific Aero Products Company in July 1916. Both B&Ws were finally sold, in 1919, to the New Zealand Flying School at Auckland—Boeing's first international sale. The two Boeings, at the time the largest aircraft in Australasia, achieved a number of altitude and distance record flights, including the first ever Royal Mail flight.

Bluebill and its sister *Mallard* were to survive until the mid-1920s but were then ignominiously burned. A replica B&W was built and flown in 1966, Boeing's 50th anniversary year, and is now preserved in the Seattle Museum of Flight.

MODEL C (later Models 3 to 5)

The earlier B&W was not found to be acceptable to the US Navy so a new improved design was started in 1916, flying for the first time in November. Given the Boeing designation of C-5 and C-6 (later Model 3), two were supplied to the navy as potential trainers. To Boeing's immense relief, an order for 50

was received with a contract value of $575,000—Boeing was in the aviation business.

To reflect this, the name of the company was changed and the Boeing Airplane Company came into existence in May 1917. The Boeing factory, formerly the Heath shipyard building, was

painted bright red, with the new name on the front. (Today that building is part of the Museum of Flight.)

Deliveries of the Model C (Model 5) began in April 1918, and were completed in November. Two additional Model Cs were built: one, designated C-1F with a single float, was for the navy; the second, the CL-4S, was to make aviation history. On March 3, 1919, William Boeing and Edward Hubbard carried the first US international airmail from Vancouver to Seattle.

ABOVE LEFT **William Boeing, holding the first US international airmail sack with his partner on the historic flight, Edward Hubbard.**

ABOVE RIGHT **Boeing's brightly painted factory, photographed in June 1918, complete with an armed guard.**

LEFT **One of the 50 Model Cs delivered to the US Navy as trainers, part of Boeing's first major military order.**

WORLD WAR I

Boeing's success in selling the Model C was to lead to other orders, but *not* for Boeing designs. At that time, when the military bought an aircraft they also bought the design rights. The designing company had to bid for any further orders in competition with other manufacturers.

With America's entry into World War I in April 1917, Boeing's factory and workforce expanded rapidly. From 28 staff in 1917, by the end of 1918 337 people were on the Boeing payroll. The factory was also enlarged to build the 50 Curtiss HS-2L seaplanes (or flying boats), which the navy had ordered in May 1918. The end of the war in November 1918 brought a rapid re-evaluation of all military orders and Boeing's HS-2L order was cut to 25.

ABOVE AND RIGHT **The large (74 feet wingspan) Curtiss HS-2L was powered by a single 360 hp Liberty engine, with the hull built of diagonal strips of wood veneer on a wooden frame. A gunner/bombardier was carried in addition to two pilots.**

LEFT **A Boeing-built DH-4M, given the naval designation of 02B-1 when used by the US Marines.**

SURVIVAL—OTHER PEOPLE'S AIRPLANES

With the completion of the 25th Curtiss, Boeing's workforce was reduced to just 80, while the company looked for other markets. Many early aircraft companies went bankrupt; those that survived, like Boeing, built whatever they could to bring in business. In Boeing's case that was furniture.

Just one airplane was to be built during 1919, but it has an important place in the Boeing story. The B-1 (later Model 6), which was, in effect, a scaled-down Curtiss HS-2L, was the first Boeing *commercial* aircraft. The sole example was sold in 1920 to Edward Hubbard, William Boeing's partner in the historic 1919 airmail flight. For eight years the B-1 carried airmail on the Seattle–Victoria (Canada) route. This historic aircraft survives to this day in the Seattle Museum of History and Industry.

A lifeline was thrown to the struggling company when, in November 1919, Boeing got a contract to rebuild 50 de Havilland DH-4 bombers. One of the few combat aircraft to be built in the USA, the 1916 British design was fitted with the American Liberty water-cooled engine. Further orders followed and over the following four years Boeing were to rebuild a total of 298 DH-4s for the US Army and Navy.

The other major contract that Boeing managed to win, in June 1921, was for 200 Thomas-Morse MB-3A fighters. This was the crucial contract, since it led to the series of famous Boeing fighters that were to secure Boeing's future.

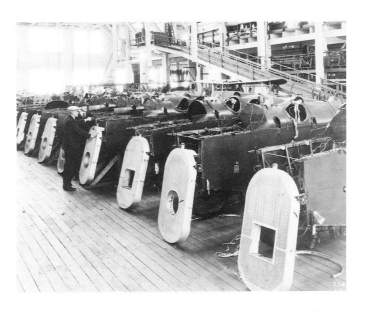

ABOVE **The Army were the main users of Boeing's rebuilt DH-4M, with its new welded steel tube fuselage.**

LEFT **Dismantled wooden DH-4 fuselages with their large radiators await rebuilding.**

MODEL LETTERS AND NUMBERS

Like most early manufacturers, Boeing did not adopt a systematic classification for its designs until the company had been in existence for a number of years. In Boeing's case, it was 1925 when a numerical system was adopted, which was also applied retrospectively to the earlier aircraft. Thus the B&W became Model 1, the various Model Cs were designated Models 3, 4, and 5, and the B-1 became Model 6. This system has been applied more or less systematically to date—at least for all designs originating in Seattle.

Usually each major modification meant a new model number. So the series of fighters that begin with Models 83 and 89 ended with model numbers between 235 and 250. Design studies for aircraft that might or might not be built were also given model numbers, which is why the sequence quickly went into the hundreds. Sometimes one model number was retained for a series of design studies —each of which was given a dash number. For example, the prototype 707 was built under model number 367-80, the 80th design concept evolved from the Model 367.

FIGHTERS, MAILPLANES, AND AIRLINERS

The first true Boeing biplane fighter, the Model 15, was to launch a family of famous fighters for both American air arms. The Army Air Corps bought the PW-9 first, followed shortly after by the navy's PB-1. The variants followed quickly, one after the other, up to the FB-5 of 1927 and the PW-9D, which were delivered during 1928. By then Boeing, with 800 employees, was one of the USA's biggest aircraft manufacturers. Replacing the heavy water-cooled Packard engine with the superb Pratt &

RIGHT Displayed in the National Air and Space Museum in Washington D.C., this historic Model 247 took third place in the 1934 England–Australia Air Race.

BELOW By December 1928 the original Heath Shipyard factory, later to be called Plant One, was already surrounded by new buildings.

BELOW A delightful shot of a Thomas-Morse MB-3A about to be delivered to the US Army during 1922. Sitting in the spare tire is Edgar Gott, then the company president.

STEARMAN TRAINERS

Whitney Wasp radial engine led to another famous pair of army and navy fighters: the P12/F4B series—of which a total of 586 were built. The first monoplane Boeing fighter, the Model 248, P-26 Peashooter, was also destined to be the last Boeing fighter to fly in the twentieth century. It served with the Army Air Corps until the outbreak of World War II.

The first Model 40 was not a success, but, as the 40A with the wonderful Wasp engine, it launched Boeing into the airmail and passenger business and into rapid expansion. The Boeing Airplane and Transport Corporation was formed as a holding company for the many other airlines, aircraft, engine, and propeller manufacturers that came into the Boeing group.

On February 1, 1929 the name was changed to the United Aircraft and Transport Corporation. In 1932 the United Air Lines, part of UATC, ordered an incredible 70 Boeing Model 247s, the world's first "modern airliner." But in 1934 new federal antitrust laws tore the whole group asunder. As aircraft manufacturers could not own mail-carrying airlines, the United Aircraft and Transport Corporation was split into three: United Air Lines, United Aircraft (now United Technologies), and the Boeing Airplane Company, including Stearman Aircraft.

Disillusioned, the founder, William Boeing, resigned his chairmanship and retired to his farm.

The tiny Stearman Company launched its Model 70 biplane trainer late in 1933. By the end of World War II no fewer than 8,548 Stearman trainers had been built. The plant at Wichita was to go on to build many of the aircraft that made Boeing the force it is today.

BELOW A colorful example of Boeing's most famous fighter, the P-26 Peashooter.

BIG BOMBERS AND WORLD WAR II

The new Boeing president, Clair Egtvedt, believed the company's future lay with big airplanes. The biggest was the experimental XB-15, but the most successful was the renowned Model 299, the B-17 Flying Fortress. From these bombers were evolved the luxurious Model 314 Clipper flying boat and the Model 307 Stratoliner. Both made prewar history. The Clipper launched scheduled transatlantic services and the Stratoliner was the world's first pressurized airliner.

But it was the bombers that ensured Boeing's fame and fortune. Although the XB-15 was built in the original Plant One, the B-17 clearly needed a new factory. This was built alongside Boeing Field on a 28-acre site. In 1936, Plant Two, as it was called, was one of the largest industrial buildings in the United States. Although the first B-29s were built in Plant One at Seattle, production was transferred to a new plant in Wichita. Like the B-17, it was also built by other manufacturers.

Boeing's workforce in the Seattle area alone grew from 1,755 in January 1938 to 8,724 by mid-1940. After Pearl Harbor and America's entry into the war, employment peaked in January

1945 at no fewer than 44,754. The ending of the war, by Boeing's B-29 bomber over the Japanese cities of Hiroshima and Nagasaki, meant the loss of 30,000 Boeing jobs in the Seattle area and more than 43,000 throughout the company.

ABOVE A unique gathering of three generations of Boeing bombers, the B-17, the B-29 (foreground) and, just visible as a 48 feet high fin, the mighty B-52. The core of the award-winning American Air Museum at Duxford, England.

LEFT In the foreground, the Wichita Plant Two, erected in the early 1940s especially to build the B-29. The original Stearman factory can be seen in the background.

RIGHT The B-17, the first of Boeing's World War II bombers. Twenty of the B-17C version seen here were delivered to the Royal Air Force as the Fortress 1.

SURVIVAL AGAIN—CARGO AIRPLANES

Boeing's new president, William Allen, took over as thousands of his employees were being laid off. The future was not quite as bleak as it had been in 1919. The company had small orders for its Model 367, the KC-97 Stratofreighter version of the B-29, and was hopeful that the commercial equivalent, the Model 377 Stratocruiser, would be a success. With comfort and luxury reminiscent of the prewar Clippers, the Stratocruiser proved too expensive when compared with the equivalent products from Douglas and Lockheed. Fortunately, the KC-97 was financially very successful. The search for its jet replacement was to bring Boeing eventual success in the commercial airline market. But first there were jet bombers.

LEFT **The portly shape of a civilianized Model 367 KC-97 freighter taxies past its famous successor, originally called the Model 367-80, better known as the 707.**

THE JET AGE—BOMBERS

On the 44th anniversary of the Wright brothers' first flight on December 17, 1903, Boeing flew its revolutionary Model 450, the B-47 Stratojet. With its swept-back wing and engines slung underneath in pods, the new jet bomber's configuration was to set the standard for almost all future Boeing jets. The B-47 became the mainstay of the Strategic Air Command, being joined, from 1955, by the mighty B-52 Stratofortress. Still in service more than 40 years later, the B-52 is likely to continue well into the twenty-first century.

RIGHT The nose of a camouflaged
B-52 frames a re-engined KC-135R.

BELOW In their natural element, a
KC-135 refuels a B-52.

THE JET AGE—AIRLINERS

Evolved from the Stratofreighter but bearing no physical resemblance, the Model 367-80 was the biggest gamble in the company's history. Serving as a prototype for both a tanker-transport successor to the Stratofreighter and for Boeing's first jet airliner, the 707, it first flew in April 1952. To build its new airliner, Boeing took over a wartime factory at nearby Renton.

The success of the long-range 707 increased the demand for jet travel from the smaller airports, which was met by the 727 tri-jet. The only rear-engined Boeing airliner, the 727 outsold its famous forebear by almost two to one, reaching a total of 1,831 by 1983. The baby Boeing airliner, the Model 737 twin jet, was designed to use even smaller airports with yet shorter runways. However, when it was launched in 1965, it was two years behind its American and British rivals and for some time it was an unwanted baby. With the 737 struggling for sales, Boeing and

BELOW To test the rear engine configuration of the 727, the 367-80 flew with a fifth engine.

Pan American World Airlines announced the world's largest airliner, the 747.

To build this giant, Boeing built a new factory 40 miles north of Seattle at Everett. The world's largest building under one roof, the Everett plant cost a fortune at the same time as the 747 was being evolved to meet Pan Am's requirements. At this time Boeing had yet another prestigious project under development: the Model 2707 Supersonic Transport—the SST. The last years of the 1960s were a critical period for Boeing with the number of employees growing rapidly to over 101,000. But income was not matching expenditure.

ABOVE At London's Heathrow Airport in 1980, a 707 of Portugal's TAP airline frames a 727 from JAT Yugoslav Airlines.

LEFT William Allen, Boeing's post World War II president, made all the critical decisions which gave the company its world leadership of the jet airliner market.

RIGHT The pillars on which Boeing's jet airliner dominance were built. The 707 (foreground) and its big brother, the 747.

BELOW The Everett Plant in the early 1970s when new 747s stood engineless awaiting their Pratt & Whitney powerplants.

OPPOSITE RIGHT Marking 20 years of the 747, on September 30, 1988, the first 747-100 flies over Seattle with number 735, the first of the new 747-400.

OPPOSITE BELOW A Boeing CH-47 Chinook of the Royal Air Force displays its agility and power.

Things got worse in the 1970s. A worldwide recession in the aviation industry meant Boeing went 18 months without a single order from a US airline. The 747 entered service in January 1970 but its engines initially proved very unreliable. While the problem was being fixed, dozens of completed 747s stood at Everett with concrete blocks on their wings instead of engines. The final blow fell in March 1971 when government funding of the SST was withdrawn, effectively canceling the Model 2707.

Boeing was $1 billion in debt and facing a bigger financial crisis than those posed by either of the postwar survival struggles. The workforce took the first blow. More than 60,000 jobs went in the Seattle area alone. No wonder a billboard on the city's outskirts read: WILL THE LAST PERSON LEAVING SEATTLE TURN OUT THE LIGHTS.

The historic Plant One, William Boeing's first factory, was sold. The 737 was being built in a new Plant Two facility. This was closed and 737 production moved into the Renton factory with the 707 and 727. By the end of 1972, Boeing had sold or shut down some 10 million square feet of office, factory, and storage space.

The medicine tasted horrible but it worked. The 747's problems were overcome, and sales of it and the 737 took off as the recession diminished. By 1983 over a thousand 737s had

been sold. Two new models, the 767 and 757, were launched almost simultaneously, with roll-outs in August 1981 and January 1982 respectively. A new advanced version of the 747, the -400, was flown in 1988 and by 1990 the 737 exceeded the 727's production record, when number 1,833 was rolled out. Four years later, the 777 joined the family of Boeing airliners. Sized between the 767 and the 747, it was the first to be wholly computer-designed.

HELICOPTERS

The acquisition, in 1960, of Vertol brought helicopters into the Boeing product line. Founded by Frank Piasecki, the Piasecki Helicopter Corporation became the Vertol Aircraft Corporation in 1955. From a revolutionary twin rotor helicopter first flown in 1945, a line of advanced helicopters were built for the US Army and Navy during the 1950s. Their replacement appeared in 1958 as the Vertol Model 107.

A successful civil helicopter, the 107, was developed for the US Navy as the CH-46 Sea Knight and as the Model 114 CH-47 Chinook for the US Army. Both helicopters were essential tools during the Vietnam War and advanced versions of the Chinook remain in production.

INTO THE NEXT MILLENNIUM

In the 1990s Boeing became involved in a number of very advanced projects and by merger and acquisition became the largest aerospace company in the world.

In partnership with Bell, Boeing is developing the multiservice V-22 Osprey tilt-rotor—a cross between the helicopter and a conventional turboprop aircraft. The US Marine Corps is expecting to receive its first aircraft early in the twenty-first century. A marginally more conventional helicopter—albeit with stealth technology—is the RAH-66 Comanche. Boeing's partner on this very advanced battlefield reconnaissance helicopter is Sikorsky—part of United Technologies, the successor to United Aircraft of 1934. The first Comanche flew in January 1996.

Lockheed, Boeing, and General Dynamics jointly built the two YF-22 prototypes in competition with the YF-23, the product of Northrop and McDonnell Douglas. The YF-22 was judged the winner and is now in the preproduction, engineering,

and manufacturing-development phase with 11 aircraft being built. When this program is completed in the early 2000s, full production will begin. Now named the F-22 Raptor, production aircraft are scheduled to begin replacing the F-15 Eagle as the USAF's primary fighter from 2005.

Even more advanced, the project called the JSF (Joint Strike Fighter) is a Boeing-led bid for a potential 3,000-fighter contract. With its partners in Europe and the United States, Boeing is expected to fly the first JSF early in 2000 in competition with a Lockheed Martin-designed aircraft. If Boeing is successful in building the production JSF, it will be the first successful Boeing fighter since the Peashooter of the mid-1930s.

In December 1996, Boeing took over the aerospace company Rockwell International as a subsidiary, renaming it Boeing North American. Just eight months later, Boeing and McDonnell Douglas merged to create a company with over 220,000 employees. Under the overall title of the Boeing Company, it is now organized into three groups:

BELOW For the first time the revolutionary Bell Boeing V-22 Osprey gives the helicopter high speed as well as vertical takeoff. The first customer is the US Marines.

- **The Information, Space, and Defense Systems Group**, which includes all military aircraft and missiles, space vehicles, rockets and engines, and aircraft information systems

- **The Boeing Commercial Airplane Group**, which has all the current Boeing airliners from 737 to 777 and the McDonnell Douglas aircraft still in production

- **The Shared Services Group**, providing computing, telecommunications, and other support services to the whole company

The products of the new company cover almost every conceivable military and civil application. Military aircraft include the F/A-18 Hornet, the AH-64 Apache, the C-17 Globemaster III, the AV-8B Harrier II, and the T-45 Goshawk. The civil aircraft include the present Boeing range plus the new Boeing 717, originally the McDonnell Douglas MD-95.

The joint commercial aircraft statistics of the Boeing Company are staggering. A total of 14,098 commercial jet airliners had been ordered since the first 707 order through to October 31, 1998. That total is made up of 1,010 707s; 1,831 727s; 4,193 737s; 1,288 747s; 942 757s; 848 767s; 428 777s; 55 717s; 556 DC-8s; 976 DC-9s; 1,325 MD 80s and 90s; 446 DC-10s, and 200 MD 11s. Of the total order book, over 12,300 had been delivered with the 717, 737 to 777, plus the MD11, MD80, and MD90 still in production. More than 9,000 Boeing Company commercial jet airliners are in service worldwide.

For the first time in its history, Boeing is facing serious competition from outside the USA, in the shape of the European Airbus consortium. Also partly as a result of its purchase of McDonnell Douglas in 1997, in that year the company recorded a net deficit of $178 million. The severe recession in the Far East has meant customer airlines canceling or deferring delivery, giving rise to some three dozen unsold Boeings being stored in the dry climate of the Arizona desert. Suffering from the growing pains of assimilating McDonnell Douglas, the Commercial Aircraft Division was reorganized late in 1998 into three business units: the single-aisle (narrow-body) airplane, the twin-aisle (wide-body) airplane, and the customer-services unit. The workforce, as usual, was also cut as a response to the crisis with at least 20,000 jobs being lost. Despite these problems, the group delivered 563 new commercial aircraft in 1998.

For the future, Boeing has been looking at a successor to the 747 for some time. The VLA (Very Large Aircraft) could be a further stretch of the 747, giving a maximum capacity of 650 to 700 passengers or even a completely new aircraft. Integrating such a large aircraft into the existing airports would be both expensive and difficult. The possibility of a replacement for Concorde is still being studied but a go-ahead looks unlikely in the immediate future. More feasible is a small, low-cost jet liner for the light-traffic or high-frequency short-range market. Which one of these, if any, is built will depend on their forecast economic viability, but Boeing is sure to remain at the forefront of commercial aviation in the new millennium.

BELOW The latest Boeing jetliner, the Model 717, formerly the MD-95, is the outcome of the 1997 merger with McDonnell Douglas.

CHAPTER TWO

FIGHTERS AND TRAINERS

LEFT Painted in the standard army olive-drab camouflage, one of the last 50 Thomas-Morse MB-3As built by Boeing during 1922.

ABOVE The first Boeing-designed pursuit aircraft, the PW-9 in its early XPW-9 version.

272-B
12-4-22

Boeing got into designing fighters almost by accident. In the financially desperate years following the end of World War I, Boeing won an Air Corps contract to build the Thomas-Morse MB-3. This experience, coupled with knowledge of the best in German fighter design, led to a belief that a better fighter could be designed and built. Persuading the military to spend their very limited allocations on new aircraft was another matter. Boeing's persistence finally paid off and, for more than decade, the Seattle aircraft manufacturer led the country in the design and production of single-seat fighters—or "pursuits," as they were then called.

It was the acquisition in the early 1930s of the small Stearman Aircraft Company that was to make Boeing the biggest producer of primary trainers for the army and navy by the end of the decade.

THE THOMAS-MORSE MB-3A

Most combat aircraft built and used by the US military during World War I were of European origin. In response to a specification issued to the US aircraft industry in the spring of 1918, Thomas-Morse designed the MB-3. Although the war was actually over when the prototype flew, the company was given an initial order for 50. The practice at the time was to seek competitive bids for subsequent contracts and thus, in 1921, Boeing was successful in its tender to build 200 improved MB-3As for the army.

The design was strongly influenced by the French Spad fighter series, being primarily of wooden construction, wire-braced, and fabric-covered. This gave rise to many problems in service and gave William Boeing food for thought during the production run that was completed by the end of 1922.

ABOVE The cockpit of a Thomas-Morse MB-3A with its unusual side mounted instruments which must have been very difficult to read.

LEFT Almost certainly the first Boeing-built MB-3A about to be collected by its army pilot. On his right is William Boeing with Edgar Gott nearest the propeller.

LEFT Production of the FB-5 during 1927, giving a good impression of its size as Boeing workers prepare for covering the fuselage with fabric.

BELOW One of the early PW-9s, with its 425 hp Curtiss D-12 engine driving a two bladed propeller, made its first flight in 1923.

MODEL 15, THE PW-9, AND THE FB

A number of Fokker D.VII fighters, the most advanced German design of World War I, were acquired by the victorious Allies at the end of the war in Europe. Dissatisfaction with the construction of the MB-3A led Boeing engineers to examine an example of the D.VII. They were very impressed by the welded-steel fuselage and wooden box wing spars. The decision was made to design a Boeing fighter.

Under the Boeing Model 15 (see page 35 for explanation of military numbers and letters), the new design was finished by January 1922. Construction of a prototype started as a wholly company-funded project—a brave decision for a small, financially struggling company. Especially as the design broke away from all the standard, army-approved methods of construction. The fuselage was built with a framework of welded-steel tubes—not the gas welding of the Fokker but a new electric-arc welding, developed by Boeing. The wings had built-up wooden spars of mixed spruce and mahogany timber, tapered in thickness toward the tips.

The army was impressed by the design and agreed to test the aircraft in competition with new designs from Fokker (Dutch-built) and Curtiss. After the first Model 15 had flown in June 1923, the Air Corps ordered two more in September 1923, as the XPW-9. However, simultaneously, they ordered 25 Curtiss fighters. Both aircraft used the Curtiss D-12 water-cooled engine, giving nearly 400 hp, and the all-Curtiss design appeared to be favorite for the large order.

After a nail-biting 12 months, in September 1924, to Boeing's immense relief, the army ordered 12 PW-9s plus a further 18 in December. Boeing was in the fighter business. The PW-9 was to establish a dynasty of single-seat pursuit aircraft which were to provide the main source of income for Boeing for the next 10 years.

The FB-1 was the navy version of the PW-9 and a total of 16 were ordered for delivery during December 1925. The majority were used by the Marine Corps, some in an expeditionary force to China in June 1928.

The army and navy versions were developed through various improvements and spanned Boeing model numbers up to the PW-9D and the Model 67—the FB-5. The latter was the last of the FB series, delivery of the 27 ordered being undertaken on January 21, 1927. The delivery process of the aircraft was somewhat unusual. They had to be moved sideways through the narrow factory doors, loaded onto nearby barges and ferried directly out to the waiting aircraft carrier USS *Langley* in Seattle Harbor.

The power plant of the FB-5 was a Packard 520-hp, inverted, water-cooled engine, which gave the fighter a top speed of 175 m.p.h. Despite its undoubted merits, the aircraft was destined to be retired from service within two years, solely due to the navy's decision to standardize on air-cooled radial engines. The PW-9D lasted longer in Army Air Corps service. The 16 delivered during April and May 1928 remained in service until 1934. A total of 114 Model 15/PW-9 fighters had been built, together with 49 of the FB series.

MODELS 69 AND 77, THE F2B AND THE F3B

The first Model 69—navy designation XF2B-1—was built by Boeing as a company-funded prototype to use the new Pratt & Whitney R-1340 Wasp air-cooled radial engine. The aircraft had many features in common with the earlier FB series. With a top speed of 154 m.p.h., 32 were ordered by the navy, with deliveries beginning in January 1928. Shortly after, the revised F3B-1 went into production with 74 ordered, first entering service in August 1928 aboard the US Navy carriers *Saratoga, Lexington,* and *Langley.* Most had been replaced in the front-line units by 1932 but continued in support duties for many years. The cost of each F3B-1 was $11,470 plus the cost of government-furnished equipment such as armament.

LEFT A rare survivor of the early Boeing fighter or pursuit, a PW-9D in the USAF Museum at Wright-Patterson Air Force Base, Ohio.

BELOW An unusual, if not unique method of delivery. With no pre-delivery test flight, four FB-5s are taken straight from the factory onto a barge to the aircraft carrier waiting in Seattle harbor.

MODELS 83 AND 89, THE FAMOUS F4B, AND THE P-12 SERIES

Destined to be built in greater numbers (586) than any other Boeing fighter series, the first Model 83 was, yet again, a company-funded project. There was nothing new or radical about the new fighter but it incorporated all Boeing's experience gained in seven years of designing and building fighters. It was also destined to be Boeing's last biplane single-seat pursuit aircraft.

Intended as a replacement for the PW-9 and F2B/F3B then in service, the first Model 83 flew in June 1928, followed in July by the Model 89. The two aircraft were virtually identical and both were given the navy designation of XF4B-I. While on test by the navy, one was loaned to the army for evaluation, resulting in orders from both services. The first, as Model 102—army designation P-12—was delivered to the Air Corps in February 1929. Navy deliveries, as Model 99, started in June 1929. Commercial and export versions were built as Model 100s. All were powered by different versions of Pratt & Whitney's reliable R-1340 Wasp radial engine.

The navy F4Bs were developed through numerous variants up to the F4B-4, which remained in squadron service aboard US carriers until 1937. Even then, the F4B continued on shore duties, including use as radio-controlled drones, until 1941.

Initially four Model 100s were built, one being delivered to what is now the Federal Aviation Agency (FAA); another went to Pratt & Whitney as an engine test bed. This aircraft is now in the Museum of Flight in Seattle. The third Model 100 was initially

ABOVE In front of the Boeing hangar, the second F4B-I for the navy carries out pre-delivery bomb load trials.

RIGHT Wooden wings and a tubular aluminum fuselage of a P-12 shows the typical construction of a Boeing fighter of the late 1920s.

RIGHT The USAF Museum's beautifully restored Boeing P-12E in the colorful markings of the 6th Pursuit Squadron with which it served in Hawaii during the 1930s.

BELOW An illustration of a Boeing F4B-1 flown by the VF-5B squadron aboard *USS Lexington* in the early 1930s.

used by Boeing before being sold to the famous stunt and racing pilot Paul Mantz in 1936 for air-show and film duties. It is now preserved in Florida. A special two-seat version was built for Howard Hughes—the industrialist turned recluse, who was also an aviator—and, after many modifications for air-show work, crashed in 1957. Two Model 100Es were sold to Thailand; one still survives in the Thai Aeronautical Museum in Bangkok after being flown by the Japanese during World War II.

The army's P-12s were improved in parallel with the F4B, up to the 500 hp P-12E with a top speed of 160 m.p.h. The prototype for the P-12E was sold to China as the Model 218. There it was flown by an American volunteer pilot who is credited with destroying two Japanese fighters before being shot down over Shanghai in 1932. The P-12E was the most widely used of all the P-12 versions, remaining in service until 1934–5 when they were replaced by the P-26 Peashooter.

RIGHT One of America's most famous airmen, then Captain Ira C. Eaker, in front of his special P-12. Later, as General Eaker, he was to be the first commander of the wartime mighty Eighth Air Force.

BELOW The civilian equivalent of the P-12/F4B was the Model 100. The second aircraft, seen here, was used by Pratt & Whitney as a flying test bed for its engines.

MODEL 248, THE P-26 PEASHOOTER

Unlike names such as Monomail and Flying Fortress, which were officially applied to Boeing aircraft, Peashooter was always an informal nickname given to the P-26 by its pilots. However, the name stuck and few now use the formal army designation. The Peashooter's place in history is assured as the Army Air Corps' and Boeing's first monoplane fighter. It was also destined to be the last fighter wholly designed by Boeing.

Designed, again, at Boeing's expense, but incorporating ideas from both Boeing and the army, the first of the three XP-936 prototypes flew in March 1932. It was redesignated XP-26, and tests showed such an improvement over the army's P-12s that an order for 111 (increased to 136) was placed in January 1933. This was the largest single army contract since 1921. The P-26, while offering innovations such as the monoplane wing and wing flaps to reduce landing speeds, had nevertheless many biplane features: wire-braced wings, open cockpit, and a fixed undercarriage enclosed in streamlined fairings. The monoplane fighter of World War II had yet to arrive.

Entering service in 1934, the P-26 was an immediate favorite with its pilots. For many years until 1938, it was the fastest pursuit in the Air Corps and many pilots who were to achieve high rank and fame in the forthcoming conflict started their service lives on the Peashooter.

No US Army Air Corps P-26 saw service in World War II having been declared obsolete by 1941. However some were sold to the Philippines, where one was credited with destroying two Japanese aircraft during the first attacks on the islands.

Two Peashooters have survived, one in the Planes of Fame Museum in California and the other in the National Air and Space Museum, Washington, DC.

THE BOEING-STEARMAN MODELS 70 TO 76

At the height of the 1930s' worldwide economic depression, the tiny Wichita-based Stearman Aircraft Company (a subsidiary of Boeing) designed and built a biplane trainer as a privately funded project. At a time when military planners were beginning to consider the monoplane for most roles, the biplane was still the preferred choice for a trainer. From the sole Model 70 came a family of primary trainers on which most American and many British Royal Air Force pilots of World War II were to gain their wings.

Both the army and the navy tested the Model 70 during March and April 1934, but initially only the navy placed an order, which was for 61 Model 73s as the Stearman NS-1 (N for trainer and S for Stearman).

Fitted with the Wright R-780 220-hp engine (the navy had a large surplus stock of this relatively old engine), deliveries were completed by 1936. Export orders for the Model 73 were received from the Phillipine and Cuban Air Forces.

The Model 75, which appeared in 1936, was to be the most successful version of the family. In that year it attracted its first army order for just 26 aircraft as PT-13, with the Lycoming R-680 220-hp engine. Repeated army orders for the PT-13 came regularly up to 1940, when a change was made to the

ABOVE **The agility of the "Stearman" is demonstrated in this low level display by a post-war civilian registered aircraft, but in the colorful pre-war training markings.**

Continental R-670 engine, also 220 hp. The airframe was unchanged, but the new engine gave rise to a new designation of PT-17. The Army Air Force bought no fewer than 3,519 of this version.

A shortage of the Continental engine brought yet another version, the PT-18, with a Jacobs R-755 engine; only 150 PT-18s were built. The final army version was the PT-27, which were supplied to the Royal Canadian Air Force as the Kaydet. Basically a PT-17, but a number had extra winter protection in the form of a canopy over the cockpits.

Navy orders closely paralleled those for the army. The PT-17 became the N2S-1, the Lycoming-engined version being designated N2S-2. Eventually, commonality between the two services was achieved in 1942 with the N2S-5/PT-13D (Boeing Model E-75), powered by the Lycoming R-680. The navy received over three-quarters of the 1,768 built.

The Model 76 designation was applied to export versions of the Model 75, fitted with armament and more powerful engines. A total of 78 were constructed prior to America's entry into World War II. Argentina, the Philippines, Brazil, and Venezuela were the recipients.

Stearman Aircraft became a division of Boeing Airplanes during World War II and the manufacturer's plate on the wartime aircraft reads "Boeing Model 75." However, the ubiquitous trainer was always known as the Stearman and, when production ended in 1945, 8,584 Stearmans had been built.

Many thousands of surplus aircraft were bought privately at the end of the war, most for use as single-seat crop dusters and sprayers. Today the Stearman is cherished as an affordable "Warbird" and air-show performer. Boeing were paid between $8,000 and $10,000 for each Model 75. Today, expect to pay up to $70,000 for a good example.

RIGHT **In a number of specialist aerobatics aircraft, the original 220 hp engine was replaced by one having three times the power. The performance and noise levels were equally impressive!**

MILITARY NUMBERS AND LETTERS— WHAT DO THEY MEAN?

Throughout this book, reference is made to apparently arbitrary combinations of letters and numbers which denote the aircraft's role and the particular version. The following notes should help explain the two main systems involved and some of the designations used.

US Army and Air Force designations

The first series of US Army designations for its aircraft began in 1920, and was revised in 1924 and at infrequent intervals since then. However, all have followed a sequence giving first the type, then the model, and finally the version of the model. Prior to 1920 the army had used the manufacturer's own designations: for example, DH-4B—a de Havilland design, its fourth model, and the second variant.

In the earliest army version, the type of engine fitted was included in the designation: for instance, PW-9D—P for pursuit, W for water-cooled engine, 9 for the ninth model of the PW series, and D was the fourth variant of the PW-9.

In the 1924 revision, the engine classification was deleted and generally, with modifications, this has been the system followed to date. The main letter prefixes are:

Type symbol	Designation	Period used and remarks
A	Attack	1924–47, became B
A	Attack	1962 to date
AT	Advanced trainer	1925–47, became T
B	Bomber	1925 to date
BT	Basic Trainer	1930–47, became T
C	Cargo (transport)	1925 to date
E	special Electronic installation	1962 to date
F	Fighter	1948 to date, formerly P
H	Helicopter	1948 to date
K	tanKer	1962 to date
L	Liaison	1942–62, formerly O
O	Observation	1924–42, became L
O	Observation	1962 to date
P	Pursuit	1925–47, became F
P	Patrol	1962 to date
PT	Primary Trainer	1925–47, became T
R	Reconnaissance	1948–62, formerly F
S	antiSubmarine	1962 to date
T	Trainer	1948 to date
U	Utility	1952 to date
V	Vertical take-off and landing	1954 to date
X	special research	1948 to date
X	eXperimental; usually a prototype	1924–62, as a prefix
Y	experimental; preproduction	1924–62, as a prefix

Examples:

Boeing B-17G Manufactured by Boeing; a Bomber, the 17th Bomber in US Army Air Force Service and the seventh (G) variant of the design.

Boeing-Stearman PT-17 Manufactured by Boeing-Stearman; a Primary Trainer, the 17th Primary Trainer in US Army Air Force Service.

US Navy and Marine designations

At first glance the US Navy system appears unintelligible, but is, in fact, very logical, albeit rather complicated. The main system was adopted in 1922 and continued up to 1962, when all US military services took up the air-force designation system.

The major difference with the Navy system was the requirement to record the manufacturer: for example:

FB-5: F, a Fighter, B, the first fighter built by Boeing, -5, the fifth variant of the FB series;

XF3B-1: X, experimental prototype of an F (fighter), 3, the third fighter built by B (Boeing), while -1 is the first variant of the F3B series.

In contrast with the air-force system, the number relates to the number of the type built by the manufacturer, not to the number of the type adopted by the service.

Although the majority of the role letters were common between the air force and navy, there were some differences. The navy used:

Type symbol	Designation	Period used and remarks
F	Fighter	1922 to date
N	Trainer	1922–60
P	Patrol	1923 to date
PB	Patrol Bomber	1935–62

Military engine designations

From 1926 piston aero engines were designated by a type and size system. The first letter identified the type:

R	Radial (air-cooled)
V	Vee (liquid-cooled)

The size used the cubic capacity to the nearest 5 cubic inches. For example:

Wright R: 1820	Radial engine of 1,820 cc capacity
Lycoming R: 680	Radial engine of 680 cc capacity
Allison V: 1710	V-12 engine of 1,710 cc capacity

When the gas-turbine engine entered service, additional letters were adopted:

J	Jet turbojet
T	Turboprop or Turboshaft in helicopters
TF	Turbofan

The cubic capacity was irrelevant so the number referred to the sequence of turbine engines ordered. For example:

General Electric	J47: Jet, 47th jet engine
Pratt & Whitney	J57: Jet, 57th engine
Lycoming	T55: Turboshaft, 55th engine
Pratt & Whitney	TF33: Turbofan, 33rd engine

CHAPTER THREE

MAIL PLANES, AIRLINERS, AND FLYING BOATS

LEFT The first Boeing built solely to carry passengers, the Model 80 was powered by three Pratt & Whitney Wasp engines, later Hornet air cooled radial engines.

ABOVE Photographed above the typical mountainous territory of the San Francisco to Chicago route is a Boeing Air Transport Model 40A Mailplane.

LEFT A pair of venerable DH-4 mailplanes which were the workhorse of the US Post Office prior to the advent of the Model 40.

BELOW The rather basic open cockpit of the Model 40A. Cockpit lighting for night flying being the only improvement over its DH-4 predecessors.

The Boeing commercial aircraft in this chapter range from slow cumbersome biplanes—little different from the converted World War I bombers they replaced—to those to be seen on the eve of the jet age. One design in particular stands out from the rest: the revolutionary, mold-breaking Boeing 247, which introduced passengers to the modern airliner.

The expansion of the powerful conglomerate, United Aircraft and Transport Corporation (UA&T), during the late 1920s and early 1930s is charted, as is the political scandal over airmail contracts, which led to an Act of Congress, the dissolution of the corporation, and a threat to the whole future of Boeing.

THE BOEING MODEL 40

In 1919, William Boeing carried the first United States international airmail between Seattle and Vancouver, British Columbia (see Chapter One). Despite this early private venture, mail carrying became a government-run business, using mainly DH-4s, converted World War I bombers with the American-built, water-cooled Liberty engine. Flying mail planes in all weathers was very hazardous: of the 40 pilots initially hired by the US Post Office, three-quarters had lost their lives by 1925. More modern equipment was therefore sought. The Post Office invited tenders but specified the heavy although powerful Liberty engine. Boeing's design was the Model 40, of which just one example was purchased.

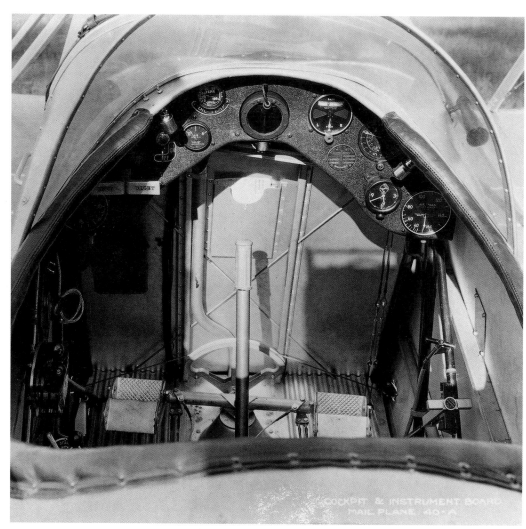

It was the advent, in 1926, of the Pratt & Whitney Wasp, producing 420 hp from its nine radial cylinders, that was to transform the Model 40 and along with it, the fledgling US airline industry.

The privatization of mail carrying was the catalyst that brought Boeing into the airline business. In 1927 they decided to bid for the San Francisco–Chicago transcontinental airmail route using the revised Model 40A. Freed from having to carry a heavy water-cooling radiator, the 40A could carry 1,200 pounds of mail (200 pounds more than the original Model 40) and two passengers. Boeing's bid of almost half that of its nearest competitor with its older equipment was eventually successful and thus Boeing Air Transport was born.

Christened *City of San Francisco* by William Boeing's wife Bertha, the first Model 40A inaugurated the new 1,918-mile service on July 1, 1927. The first passenger—an intrepid woman reporter from the Chicago *Herald-Examiner*—was carried the following day. What now takes but a few hours was then a marathon journey of 23 hours. This was, however, typical of the pioneering spirit of the age, which had seen, just six weeks before, Charles Lindbergh fly nonstop from New York to Paris, France, in 33½ hours.

Boeing Air Transport was to buy a total of 24 Model 40As from its parent company at a cost of $25,000 each.

An improved version, the Model 40B-4, with the more powerful 525-hp Pratt & Whitney Hornet, could squeeze up to four passengers into the tiny cabin forward of the pilot in his

open cockpit. Flying for the first time in October 1928, the 40B-4 remained in production until 1932 and was also built in Vancouver by the Canadian subsidiary, Boeing Canada.

Of the 81 Model 40s built, just two original examples have survived, both B-4 versions; one is in the Chicago Museum of Science and Industry, the other at Dearborn, Michigan, in the Henry Ford Museum. A replica Model 40A is also displayed in the Museum of Flight in Seattle.

ABOVE Carrying the United Air Lines logo, a Hornet engined Model 40B-4 of Pacific Air Transport awaits its four passengers and mail.

ABOVE A Model 40B operated by the Boeing Air Transport System.

MODEL 80

As William Boeing had foreseen, carrying passengers was to change from a mere adjunct to the mail service to the primary source of revenue—the mail becoming the icing on the cake. The first Boeing aircraft designed from the outset to carry passengers was the Model 80. It was a 12-passenger, three-engined biplane, and the welded-tube fuselage gave headroom for a six-foot-tall passenger. The first Model 80 flew on July 27, 1928. At a time when other manufacturers were beginning to offer monoplanes, Boeing kept to the biplane formula because of the number of small, high-altitude airports Boeing Air Transport used on its routes.

This ability to land slowly meant, regrettably, that the Model 80 was no faster than the earlier Model 40 with its single engine. Speed is always a factor when passengers are choosing which airline to travel with, and thus Boeing were to build only 16 Model 80s. This total included the improved Model 80A, in which the Wasp engines were replaced by the more powerful Pratt & Whitney Hornets, making it possible to carry up to 18 passengers.

Although not a financial success, the Model 80, during its service with Boeing Air Transport (BAT), introduced an innovation that is now an accepted part of air travel—the female flight attendant, or stewardess. Cabin attendants were not new, but female ones were. Pilots of that period had the same negative attitude to female crew members as had their naval counterparts: it was guaranteed bad luck! When eight registered nurses were employed on the San Francisco route in 1930, the overwhelming response of the passengers ensured that the three-month experiment became a permanent feature.

There was one other version of the Model 80 that deserves a special mention, heralding as it did the special "VIP" Boeings to come. Given a new model number, 226, the penultimate Model 80 was delivered to the Standard Oil Company of California in December 1930 with a luxurious executive interior. The cabin boasted deluxe features such as six adjustable, well-stuffed chairs, side and folding tables, a galley with stove, sink, and refrigerator, and even two beds.

TOP **A near full load of passengers await permission to board their Model 80A.**

ABOVE **The luxurious cabin of the "VIP" Model 226. The telephone is in use via a landline with the aircraft still on the ground.**

LEFT **Standard Oil's executive transport with special anti-drag features on the wheels and engines.**

The sole surviving Model 80 can be seen in the Seattle Museum of Flight. Abandoned in Alaska after World War II, it was recovered in 1960 from the Anchorage City garbage dump. After an extensive restoration, it was placed on display in the museum in time to mark the 50th anniversary of the introduction of the stewardess.

BELOW The pilot's cockpit of the Model 200 Monomail, showing the increased sophistication of the revolutionary new design.

MODEL 200 MONOMAIL

Boeing stayed with the biplane configuration for longer than many of its competitors for many reasons. One was undoubtedly that its main business was building military aircraft. The military were slow to accept the advantages that a single wing could provide, seeing only the disadvantages. But, when Boeing did start building monoplanes, one of the first would have almost all the features that constituted a modern airliner.

The Model 200 used the same 575-hp Pratt & Whitney Hornet engine as the Model 40B, but, with a maximum speed of 158 m.p.h., was 20 m.p.h. faster. This performance increase was achieved by a host of new radical features. The wing, with a span of 59 feet, was fully cantilevered with no external bracing wires or struts. The undercarriage retracted backward into the wing leaving just half the wheel in the airstream. A smooth semi-monocoque fuselage gave improved streamlining and a much more modern appearance. Despite these innovations, the Monomail retained the DH-4-style open cockpit with the mail carried in a compartment in front of the pilot.

Much of the potential performance increase that the new features should have produced was lost because variable-pitch propellers were not available. When the Monomail first flew in May 1930, its propeller was preset to give a compromise between that required to accelerate for the take-off and that required for high-speed flight. The best analogy is to imagine having just one gear on your car. It has to be low enough for the car to move off without stalling the engine, but the engine will be over-revving long before top speed can be reached.

BELOW The aerodynamic refinement of the revolutionary Model 200 is very apparent in this illustration of the sole example.

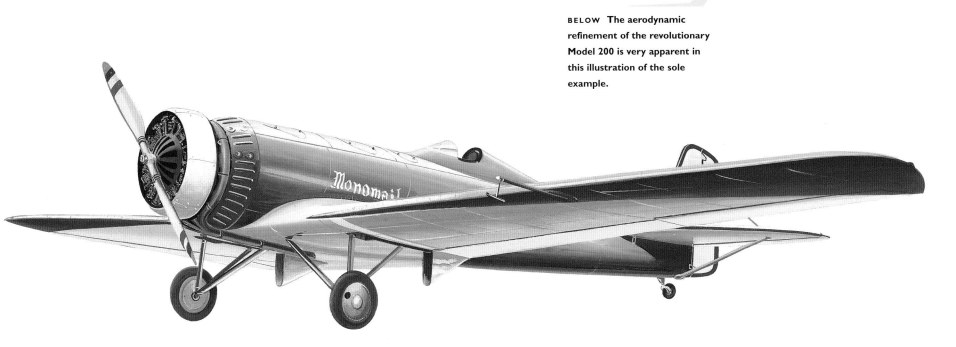

The sole Model 200 was converted to carry eight passengers as the Model 221A. A second 221 was built with a fuselage 27 inches longer to permit eight passengers to be carried separately from the 750 pounds of mail. Both machines served with Boeing Air Transport/United Airlines. Although no further Monomails were built, they were the parents of a design that would revolutionize commercial aviation.

MODEL 247

The era of the modern airliner, believe it or not, started on February 8, 1933. On that date, the first Boeing 247 made its maiden flight and overnight the world's air transport fleet was made obsolete. Although biplanes were still dominant, it was low- and high-wing monoplanes that had begun to challenge that dominance. However, the Fokker aircraft and their Ford-built equivalents had thick cantilever wings built of wood or of corrugated metal like the Junkers low-wing designs. Many had fabric-covered cabins and all had fixed undercarriages. The Boeing 247 instantly made existing airliners look slow, cumbersome, and old-fashioned.

The prototype Model 247 was a low-wing cantilever monoplane with closely cowled Pratt & Whitney Wasp radial engines, each producing 550 hp. The aircraft had an all-metal structure and its fuselage had room for 10 passengers and their baggage. With fully retractable landing gear, it could cruise at 155 m.p.h. (at least 50 m.p.h. faster than its Fokker and Ford predecessors). The range was nearly 500 miles and, unlike the tri-motors it was to replace, it could climb with a full load powered by just one engine.

Although the design incorporated many new features, it was evolutionary rather than revolutionary. The structural and aerodynamic developments Boeing had initiated in the Model 200 Monomail were incorporated into the Model 247, which was to achieve a degree of success denied to its forebears.

Initial production of the aircraft was as the Model 247, but later all aircraft were converted to the 247D standard, which had variable-pitch propellers, more powerful engines, greater range, and was the first transport to have wing and tail unit de-icing (using inflatable rubber inserts in the leading edges).

Ironically, it was the overwhelming success of the design—and the then enormous order in 1932 of 70 aircraft by the various companies that comprised United Air Lines—that was to restrict total production to only 75 machines.

AIRLINE SERVICE

United Air Lines (UAL) accepted their first Boeing 247 on March 30, 1933 and placed it into service immediately, on their United States transcontinental route. The aircraft reduced the journey time to just under 20 hours—a cut of over seven hours from the previous fastest journey. The aircraft was very popular with passengers, the only drawback was that the wing spars passed through the cabin, which caused some obstruction. They were, however, useful for the flight attendants to sit on when talking to adjacent passengers.

Airlines such as Transcontinental and Western Airlines (later Trans World Airlines, or TWA) were also anxious to order the Boeing 247 in order to remain competitive. However, Boeing, with a commitment to deliver the first 70 aircraft to UAL, could

ABOVE Also called Monomail, the Model 221 was converted from the 200 to carry six or eight passengers as well as mail.

FAR RIGHT The two steps over the wing spars are apparent in this interior view of the Model 247 cabin.

RIGHT The first Model 247 carrying the experimental registration X-13301 and the Boeing Air Transport logo.

not promise any deliveries for at least a year. Thus TWA looked elsewhere and Douglas offered the DC-1. The DC-1 led via the DC-2 to the DC-3, the airplane that more than any other established a worldwide airline network. Boeing were thus not to reap the commercial benefits that their pioneering efforts deserved. Not until the Model 707 appeared was Boeing to successfully challenge the dominance of the Douglas airliner.

One Model 247D had a particularly unusual career. Originally ordered by UAL, it was modified with long-range fuel tanks in the cabin in order to compete in the 1934 MacRobertson Air Race. Commemorating the centenary of the foundation of the Australian State of Victoria, prize money totaling £15,000 was offered by Sir MacPherson Robertson to competitors in a 12,200-mile air race from England to Melbourne, Australia. The race was won by a specialist racing machine, the de Havilland DH-88 Comet, but third overall and second in the transport category was the Boeing 247D flown by Colonel Roscoe Turner and Clyde Pangborn.

However, even this achievement was overshadowed by a Douglas machine. A DC-2 , entered by the Royal Dutch Airline KLM, carrying three passengers and mail, took second place overall and, of course, first place in the transport category. After its moment of relative glory, the 247D was returned to UAL and passed through various owners before joining the Civil Aeronautics Authority (CAA), later the Federal Aviation Agency

(FAA). After an honorable career, this historic machine finally became part of the National Air and Space Museum collection in the Smithsonian Institution in Washington, DC.

At least a further three 247s have survived, one in the Canadian National Aviation Museum in Ottawa, another in the collection of the London-based Science Museum, and the third, the only one in flying condition, in the Seattle Museum of Flight.

ABOVE The second Model 247D carrying United Air Lines livery.

THE RISE AND FALL OF UA&T

The success of Boeing Air Transport (BAT) and the Boeing Airplane Company stimulated an expansion of the business, initially by the acquisition in October 1928 of Pacific Air Transport (PAT). A parent company, Boeing Airplane and Transport Corporation (BA&T) was formed, which in February 1929 was reorganized into the United Aircraft and Transport Corporation (UA&T). This grouping of businesses, then the largest in the United States, was formed to provide the holding company for a unique gathering of many of the country's leading aviation companies.

Joining BA&T were Pratt & Whitney, who supplied most of Boeing's engines; the Hamilton Aero Manufacturing Company, provider of propellers to Boeing; the Hamilton Metal Plane Company; and Chance Vought. The pair of Hamilton companies were founded by Thomas Hamilton, who had also started his business in Seattle in 1916 before finally moving to Milwaukee in Wisconsin. The Hamilton Metal Plane Company continued to build, under the Boeing Hamilton name, the H-45, an advanced, all-metal, high-wing monoplane, just one example of which survives to this day.

Other acquisitions and mergers rapidly followed until UA&T included many of what were to become the giants of the American aviation industry. Names such as the Standard Steel Propeller Corporation of Pittsburgh, which, in January 1930, merged with Hamilton Aero Manufacturing to form the famous Hamilton-Standard propeller manufacturer; Sikorsky Aviation Corporation, then specializing in amphibians, later of course, to become the premier helicopter manufacturer; Northrop Aircraft, building mainly training aircraft; and Stearman Aircraft of Wichita. To the airline portfolio was added Stout Airlines, National Air Transport, and Varney Air Lines—all with BAT and PAT making up United Air Lines Inc.

The group also owned a number of airports and established the Boeing School of Aeronautics in Oakland, California.

In 1929 the Stock Market crashed but the UA&T's first annual report in the same year showed a profit of $8.3 million with assets of $27 million. An enormous sum in 1929. But the seeds of destruction of this Goliath were about to be sown. A meeting called by the Postmaster General, a meeting that was later to be called the "Spoils Conference," reorganized the airways map of the United States and divided up the lucrative mail contracts within the major airline groups.

Three years later, in 1933, an investigative reporter cried "Scandal!" Although Senate hearings were to clear the Postmaster General, the President, Franklin D. Roosevelt, canceled all airmail contracts and ordered that mail be flown by the Army Air Corps. Starting in February 1934, 11 pilots were killed or severely injured in the first week with eight aircraft destroyed. By March it was obvious that the mail would have to be returned to private operators, but under new regulations.

There was to be no connection between an airline and an aircraft or aero-engine manufacturer. Also, no airline executive who had attended the Spoils Conference could bid for the mail contract. This legislation totally disrupted the UA&T empire. Fortunately, it was possible for the airlines to continue under new names: United became United Air Lines Transport.

Boeing was badly hit by all of this, losing all of its subsidiaries except Stearman Aircraft and Boeing Canada. The biggest loss was that of William Boeing himself. Disillusioned, he severed virtually all his contacts with the Boeing Airplane Company, including selling all his shares. His retirement from the business at the age of 53 was a severe loss not only to Boeing but also to the whole of the American aviation industry.

BELOW LEFT The Model 40C, the last version of the design, was capable of carrying four passengers.

BELOW The two control wheels of the sole surviving Boeing Hamilton H-45 Metalplane.

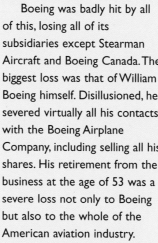

MAIL PLANES, AIRLINERS, AND FLYING BOATS

(PAA), it first flew at the end of December 1938. This prototype was to be tragically lost with all 13 passengers and crew aboard in March 1939 when a spin led to a structural failure. With an enlarged vertical tail, the first aircraft of four for Pan Am flew in August 1939. Called *Clipper Rainbow*, she and her sister aircraft flew on the Pan Am Latin American routes.

MODEL 307 STRATOLINER

To some of its detractors, the Model 307 was a converted B-17. That fails to do justice to the design, which incorporated at least one major innovation. The Stratoliner did use the wings, tail, and engines of the Flying Fortress but married to a completely new fuselage, which, uniquely for its time, offered pressurization. Thus for the first time passengers could fly above the bad weather, which often made long-distance flying so uncomfortable.

Ordered by both Transcontinental and Western Airlines (TWA—now Trans World Airlines) and Pan American Airways

With five crew and carrying up to 33 passengers, five Stratoliners served with TWA until 1942, when they were taken over by the Army Air Transport Command as C-75s. A total of only 10 Model 307s were built, but one, designated SB-307B, has a unique history. The multimillionaire Howard Hughes wished to purchase a Model 307 for a round-the-world record attempt. Boeing, with its prior commitments to TWA and PAA,

ABOVE In its Pan American Airways livery, the third Model 307 carried the US civil registration, NC 19903. It was destined to be the sole complete survivor of the ten built.

RIGHT That sole surviving aircraft, photographed in 1988, on display in the Pima County Air Museum, Tucson, Arizona when on loan from the National Air and Space Museum, Washington DC.

ABOVE Howard Hughes'
personal 307 converted to a
luxurious houseboat.

could not offer an early delivery, so Hughes, in order to secure an aircraft, bought TWA, lock, stock, and barrel. The first Model 307 of the six on order was diverted for his use.

The outbreak of World War II prevented the record flight being achieved, so it became Hughes's personal deluxe transport, but was to be little used. Damaged by a Florida hurricane, the aircraft was still virtually new, having flown just 500 hours over a 24-year period. Although the airplane was eventually scrapped, the fuselage was purchased and converted into a unique, luxurious houseboat.

One other complete Model 307 still survives. The third Pan Am machine passed through many owners—including the infamous "Papa Doc" Duvalier of Haiti—until 1967, when, with over 20,500 hours flown, it was acquired by the National Air and Space Museum. For many years it was on display at the Pima County Air Museum near Tucson, Arizona.

MODEL 314 CLIPPER

Although it had a later model number than the 307 Stratoliner, the 314 was completed earlier. Designed to meet Pan American's requirements for a long-range transoceanic flying boat, the prototype flew in June 1938. Using the wing from the XB-15, the 314 was then the largest airplane in production in the world. It was too big to be built in the old Plant One, so assembly of the airplane took place on the riverside ramp outside the factory.

With a crew of up to 10 and capable of carrying up to 74 passengers in four separate compartments on different levels—some of which could be sleeping areas—the Model 314 was the last word in luxury travel. It had, for the first time, flush toilets and could even have a full bridal suite.

Severe problems were experienced with the prototype's stability, both on the water and in the air. As with a number of Boeing designs, the tail area initially proved inadequate for directional control. The initial solution with the Model 314 was to replace the single fin and rudder with a pair, one on each end of the horizontal tail. Finally, the original fin was replaced giving a triple-fin arrangement.

Very late, the first Boeing Clipper entered service with Pan Am in May 1939, initially carrying mail. Three of the Model 314s were later sold to British Overseas Airways Corporation (BOAC) to operate a regular transatlantic service. The remaining nine aircraft were requisitioned by the US Army and Navy, although four were loaned back to PAA for its use. All nine continued to be flown by civilian crews.

Postwar, PAA briefly resumed its Model 314 service but the days of the flying boat were over as faster, four-engined land planes became available. No Boeing Clippers have survived.

ABOVE Surrounded by sea spray, the **Atlantic Clipper, Pan American's fourth Boeing Model 314,** launches into the air.

ABOVE RIGHT The problems of maintenance on the water were eased in the Model 314 by access to the rear of the engines via a passageway through the wings.

RIGHT The spacious control cabin of the 314 housed a crew of six.

MODEL 377 STRATOCRUISER

The Model 377 was the civilian equivalent of the C-97 (see Chapter Four). Both used the B-29's tail, wings, and lower fuselage with a large upper fuselage grafted on to form a double-bubble shape. As with so many Boeing aircraft, Pan Am was the launch customer, buying 20 of the 55 Stratocruisers built, the first being delivered in February 1949.

With its two decks, the Stratocruiser evoked the prewar atmosphere of spacious elegance. A separate staircase linked the upper main cabin to the lower bar and cocktail cabin. Although it was possible to carry 100 passengers the normal capacity was from 55 to 75 people. The 377 was surprisingly fast for its apparent bulk with a cruising speed of 340 m.p.h. over a maximum range of 4,200 miles.

Other customers for the Stratocruiser included BOAC, Northwest Airlines, and United Air Lines. Eight were also bought by American Overseas Airlines (AOA), which became part of the PAA fleet when AOA was taken over. BOAC became the second largest operator, buying six new and a further 11 used 377s.

Only 55 Stratocruisers were built largely because of the high cost of $1.75 million, compared with approximately $1 million for the competing Douglas DC-6 and Lockheed Constellation. Without the military C-97 program, Boeing would have made a massive loss on the 377 but it did serve to keep Boeing in the commercial airliner business.

ABOVE This is not an oversized overhead locker! In a more elegant age, long overnight flights in the 377 were eased by a limited number of sleeping bunks.

LEFT Fitted with a chin mounted radar similar to the military KC-97, this Stratocruiser nears the end of its useful life.

RIGHT **Developed from
redundant Model 377s, four
Super Guppies were used by
Airbus Industrie in Europe to
carry oversized aircraft
components.**

BELOW **The nose of a Guppy
swings open to reveal a pair of
Airbus wings.**

THE GUPPIES

The Stratocruiser's double-bubble fuselage lent itself to some of
the most extreme modifications ever inflicted on an aircraft.
Aero Space Lines had a contract to transport rocket sections
across America. They were too large for road or rail, so sea was
the only option—until the first "Pregnant Guppy" was produced.
The fuselage was lengthened by nearly 17 feet and a new upper
bubble, 20 feet high, was inserted. The cargo was loaded by
unbolting the complete rear of the fuselage behind the wing.

Given the designation 377-PG (Pregnant Guppy), the first
was so successful that production of 10 Super Guppies was
initiated. Fitted with Pratt & Whitney turboprops producing
5,700 hp, the 377-SG was even bigger, capable of carrying a
cargo up to 25 feet in diameter; the nose was modified to swing
open, facilitating loading.

Airbus Industrie in France needed a large cargo carrier to
transport fuselage sections of its Airbus designs around Europe.
The Super Guppy met this need and Airbus bought four. It is
ironic that the Airbus, which is now Boeing's biggest competitor,
found a Boeing aircraft essential for its business.

CHAPTER FOUR

BOMBERS, TANKERS, AND FREIGHTERS

LEFT With the stunning backdrop of the 14,410 feet high Mount Rainier, a production B-17E displays the new ball turret, the first to be fitted to a Flying Fortress.

ABOVE The very successful freighter developed from the B-29 bomber, the KC-97 Stratofreighter, was the military version of the civil Stratocruiser.

ABOVE Only one XB-15 was
built, but it proved that Boeing
could design and build good Big
Bombers.

Boeing in the mid-1930s was actually financially
struggling. The Depression was at its height and the
company was also suffering from the debacle that followed the
government-forced dismemberment of the once mighty United
Aircraft and Transport. However, as ever in a crisis, Boeing was
looking to the future and was prepared to stake almost
everything on what it believed was the right airplane. Boeing
was thinking of Big Bombers. This train of thought was to lead to
the immortal B-17 Flying Fortress and the mighty B-29 Superfortress—but first there was the XB-15, the biggest of them all.

MODEL 294, THE XB-15

In 1935, Boeing won an Army Air Corps contract to build a
"long-range airplane suitable for military purposes." This giant
was then the largest and heaviest aircraft built in the USA. It
finally flew in October 1937. With a wingspan of almost 150 feet
and weighing nearly 38,000 pounds empty, it dwarfed everything
around it. The wing was so thick that a passageway was provided
so that the accessories at the rear of the engines could be
serviced in flight.

The design achieved its objective, having an exceptionally
long range of over 5,000 miles, and the XB-15 also set several
world records for carrying loads. In July 1939, for example, it
carried a payload of over 71,000 pounds to an altitude of 8,200
feet. However, even four 1,000 hp Pratt & Whitney R-1830 Twin
Wasp radial engines proved insufficient to give a satisfactory
performance in such an enormous aircraft.

The sole XB-15 was used for research and development by
the Army Air Corps before being converted in 1943 to the XC-
105 transport. It served in the Pacific for the rest of the war,

carrying troops and cargo. Although the XB-15 was
ignominiously scrapped at the end of World War II, many of its
design features nevertheless appeared in the B-17, the B-29, and
the Model 314 Clipper; but, most important, it proved that
Boeing could build good, big airplanes.

MODEL 299, B-17 FLYING FORTRESS

Unlike the XB-15, which was funded by the Army Air Corps, the
Model 299 was designed and built entirely at Boeing's expense.
Initially $275,000 was allocated to the project. It was the
company's response to an Air Corps specification for a multi-
engined bomber capable of carrying 2,000 pounds of bombs,
2,000 miles at 200 m.p.h.

The specification arrived at a time when the design team
was already at work on the Model 294 (XB-15) so, not
unnaturally, the Model 299 appeared as a scaled-down version
of its larger "older" brother. (In fact, the first B-17 flew more
than two years before the XB-15.) Although four-engined
bombers were not unknown, it was generally accepted that
multi-engined meant two engines. This configuration was chosen
by both the Douglas and Martin companies, Boeing's
competitors in the forthcoming competition.

The first Model 299 was unveiled to the world in July 1935,
gleaming in its polished aluminum finish. The aircraft appeared as
an all-powerful silver giant to the press and invited guests. With
a crew of eight, and four defensive machine-gun positions, it was
a local Seattle newspaperman who is credited with the
immortal words, "She's a Flying Fortress." The name stuck and
eventually Boeing patented the description as the official title of
their most famous bomber.

That fame was far in the future and looked most unlikely
when, in October 1935, the sole Model 299 crashed during its
army trials, thus effectively eliminating Boeing from the
competition. This was a devastating blow to the struggling
company. The final cost of building the Model 299 had been
over $430,000, a massive sum for a small (600 employees)
airplane manufacturer. It appeared that the gamble had not paid
off and the future looked very bleak.

Fortunately, the cause of the accident was found to be no
fault of the aircraft and the partially completed trials had shown
the great potential of the new Boeing. Failure to complete the
trials, however, meant that Douglas, with their B-18 Bolo (based
on the DC2), won the competition and won orders totaling 350.

Boeing received a very slender lifeline with an order for just
13 Model 299Bs under the designation YB-17. The revised
aircraft differed from the first machine primarily in the

replacement of the Pratt & Whitney Hornet engines by the Wright nine-cylinder R-1820 Cyclone radial engine, giving 1,000 hp at take-off. Fitted with turbo superchargers, this engine, developed with ever-increasing horsepower, was to power all the remaining versions of the B-17.

Boeing's financial overcommitments were growing worse since the original Boeing factory—now Plant One—was far too small to construct both the XB-15 and the B-17. A new factory, Plant Two, was built adjacent to Boeing Field, providing a modern, spacious assembly building which is still in use today.

INTO SERVICE

Twelve of the first 13 B-17s were delivered during 1937 to equip the 2nd Bombardment Group; the 13th went for army development trials. The crews of the 2nd Bombardment Group set about making a name for themselves and their new bomber. They staged a spectacular demonstration flight by six aircraft to Buenos Aires and back. Thus the B-17 proved itself to be superior to its competitors but the Air Corps had already placed large orders for the Douglas machine. They could not afford to buy expensive Boeings costing almost twice as much. Additional orders dribbled through for 39 B-17Bs but, despite the impeding world conflict, the cost of the B-17 was almost to kill the whole program.

ABOVE The gleaming prototype Model 299 is revealed for the first time and is hailed as a "Flying Fortress."

LEFT New York had its first view of the Flying Fortress in 1937 when the 96th Bombardment Squadron took its YB-17s over the city.

Late in 1939, the Army Air Corps was negotiating to buy 38 B-17Cs but refused to pay the $205,000 that Boeing had fixed as the original cost of each aircraft. This price had then been based on an assumption that the company would win the contract for 200-plus aircraft. It had been losing money on each B-17 it had sold since 1936. The army refused to pay more than $198,000 and, not unreasonably, Boeing could not accept even bigger losses. In the first six months of 1939, the company had already lost $2.6 million. Its order books were very sparse with just the remainder of the B-17B order, six Model 314s for Pan Am, plus 250 Boeing Stearman trainers from the Stearman plant in Wichita. Finally, in the spring of 1940, the impasse was broken with Boeing agreeing to a $2,500 price cut, paid for by deleting items such as the external bomb racks.

This, at the time when Europe was in flames and war was shortly to engulf the rest of the world!

When, in December 1941, the attack on Pearl Harbor brought the United States into World War II, the Army Air Corps had approximately 100 B-17s in service. Many were destroyed on the ground in the first few hours of the attacks on Hawaii and the Philippines, but these were not the first Flying Fortresses to see action.

ROYAL AIR FORCE SERVICE

Under the designation Fortress Mark I, No. 90 Squadron, Royal Air Force, had started operations from a new airfield in central England, RAF Polebrook, in July 1941. (Polebrook was destined to be the home of B-17s for longer than any other UK airfield, because in June 1942, it became the home of the 97th Bomb Group, the vanguard of what became the mighty Eighth Air Force.) These first sorties highlighted the operational deficiencies of the early Flying Fortress and led to significant changes, which made all subsequent B-17s visually different from those that had gone before. Despite the description of Flying Fortress, daylight operations by the RAF proved that the defensive armament was inadequate. All seven machine guns were manually operated but the largest defect was the total lack of tail guns, which meant the crew were defenseless against an attack from directly behind.

TOP Prewar B-17s all had a highly polished bare aluminum finish.

ABOVE The first operational use of the B-17 was by the RAF in July 1941.

RIGHT The captain's control wheel and main instrument panel of an airworthy B-17G, still flying regularly for airshows and movie work.

/BELOW **A narrow catwalk between vertical racks of bombs in the bomb bay links the flight deck to the radio room.**

IMPROVED AIRCRAFT

Thus it was that the B-17E appeared late in 1941 with a much enlarged tail unit to improve directional stability at high altitudes, a manually operated, twin-gun tail position, and power-operated turrets, positioned above and below the fuselage. There were a total of 13 machine guns—all but one being of half-inch caliber. Now it was truly a Flying Fortress. The crew had also grown to at least 10 men.

Operational experience over Europe was eventually to produce the final "G" model B-17 with a power-operated nose turret to counter head-on attacks. Now all 13 guns were of half-inch caliber.

LEFT **A wartime crew await the order to board their well-worn B-17F for another hazardous daylight mission over Germany.**

BELOW **A new B-17F carries external bomb racks under its wings.**

THE MIGHTY EIGHTH

Although B-17s were used in all American theaters of war, it was the 8th Army Air Force (the Mighty Eighth) of the US Army Air Corps that was the primary operator. Based in eastern England from 1942 to the end of the war, the 8th was charged with the task of daylight strategic bombing, attacking the enemy's industry and combat capability.

The B-17 equipped two of the three Bombardment Divisions that made up the 8th Air Force. The Third Division operated the Consolidated B-24 Liberator. Each bomber has its devotees but, when a crew had flown both aircraft, the B-17 was always their first choice.

FAR LEFT Two B-17 gunners at the waist positions. They are wearing bulky clothing to protect against the bitter cold at high altitude.

LEFT Introduced after combat experience by the RAF B-17 crews, the tail gunner protects the aircraft from rear attack.

BELOW Boeing employees at Seattle covered the 5,000th Flying Fortress with their signatures.

From small beginnings with the 97th Bomb Group in the summer of 1942, just one group of three squadrons with some 40 aircraft had grown by May 1945 to 26 groups flying the B-17 and a further 14 groups of B-24s. In addition, there were another 15 fighter groups providing escort protection to the bombers.

Of the three versions of the B-17—the E, F, and G models— the last was the most numerous. Some 6,500 B-17Gs were assigned to the 8th Army Air Force with a peak strength reached in March 1945 of around 2,370. A total of 1,301 were lost in action, each carrying a crew of 10 men.

B-17 memorials

The B-17 appears on many memorials to the men of the Mighty Eighth erected at or near their bases in England. Some take the form of a stained-glass window in the local church while others— normally on the old, now disused, airfield—are impressive stone tablets. A unique surviving relic in the form of a large painting of a B-17 is *The Big Picture* which used to decorate the wall of a crew room at the Podington Air Base of the 92nd Bomb Group in south-central England. It is now preserved at the Imperial War Museum, Duxford Airfield, near Cambridge.

The Mighty Eighth is the title of the first of a trilogy, written by the renowned author Roger A. Freeman. These books are recognized as the definitive history of the Eighth Army Air Force in Europe during World War II.

LEFT The young crew of a B-17G of the 388th Bombardment Group, pose self-consciously for the camera.

BELOW Members of the Eighth Wall Art Conservation Society discuss how to preserve The Big Picture.

LEFT The memorial window to the 384th Bombardment Group in the village church of Grafton Underwood, Northamptonshire, England.

		YB-17 (1936)	B-17G (1944)
Engines	9-cylinder, radial	Wright R-1820-39 1,000 hp 850 hp at 5,000 ft	Wright R-1820-97 1,200 hp
Crew		Six	Ten
Dimensions	wing span length height	103 ft 9 in 68 ft 4 in 18 ft 4 in	103 ft 9 in 74 ft 4in 19 ft 1 in
Weights	empty fully loaded	24,458 lb 42,600 lb	36,135 lb 65,500 lb
Performance	maximum speed cruising speed service ceiling range	246 m.p.h. 217 m.p.h. 30,000 ft 1,380 miles	287 m.p.h. 182 m.p.h. 35,600 ft 2,000 miles
Armament	machine guns maximum bomb load	5 × 0.3 in 10,500 lb	13 × 0.5 in 17,600 lb

PRODUCTION

A total of 12,731 B-17s were built, with production divided among Boeing in Seattle, the Douglas Aircraft Company in Long Beach, California, and the Lockheed (Vega) Aircraft Corporation in Burbank, also in California. Of the total, Lockheed built 2,750 and Douglas, 2,995. (Their B-18 Bolo, obsolete as a bomber by 1941, was used largely in training and transport roles.) At the peak of production in June 1944, Boeing's Plant Two was rolling out 16 Flying Fortresses every 24 hours.

The B-17G of 1944 was very different than the first YB-17, as the comparative specifications (shown left) demonstrate.

SPECIAL VERSIONS

Although the B-17G was the last production version of the Fortress, throughout its service life special versions had been built. These included the XB and YB-40, conceived as bomber escorts. These B-17s had 14 power-driven machine guns, including an extra turret in the radio compartment. The ammunition load varied between 11,000 and 17,000 rounds. The concept failed because the heavily loaded aircraft could not keep up with its charges on the return flight after they had dropped their bombs.

Other special versions were:

- XC-108s, converted transports, mainly former F models

- F-9, not a fighter, but photo-reconnaissance (fighters were P for Pursuit)

- PB-1, US Navy versions of the B-17G, used for air-sea rescue but also as the PB-1W for antisubmarine work

- B-17H, the Army Air Corps search-and-rescue version with an air-droppable lifeboat

- QB-17L, an expendable target drone (in 1960, the last one in service was destroyed by an IM-99 Bomarc anti-aircraft missile—designed and built by Boeing!).

LEFT **With camouflage no longer a requirement in Europe, these 16 silver Flying Fortresses represent just one day's production in April 1944.**

Postwar, the overwhelming majority of B-17s were scrapped, but a number were converted to airliners, aerial-survey craft, and later, water bombers to fight forest fires. Today a handful of B17s are still being flown as historic aircraft for air-show displays and movie work. Most surviving examples of the plane are now in museums, where their incredible history is recorded for future generations.

MODEL 345, B-29 SUPERFORTRESS

What finally became the B-29 was first conceived in 1938 as a pressurized B-17 with a tricycle undercarriage. What was eventually built to meet an army requirement issued in 1940 was a very different "superbomber." The design was so impressive that, incredibly, the army placed an order for 250 in May 1941, more than 15 months before the first B-29 flew.

LEFT Three of the five B-17s which were gathered in England during 1989 for the remake of the renowned wartime documentary movie *The Memphis Belle*.

BELOW Fourteen pre-production B-29s were built to test all the aircraft's complicated systems as fast as possible. This is number seven.

maximum output of 2,200 hp. This new, unproved powerplant fitted with two turbochargers was to be the Achilles heel of the mighty B-29 and to lead to early tragedy.

The development program of the XB-29 was dogged by repeated engine failures: it is recorded that one of the two prototypes in just 27 tours of test flying had 16 engines and 22 carburetor changes. This appalling record culminated in a disastrous in-flight engine fire in the second XB-29, which burned through the wing before an emergency landing could be made. Boeing's chief pilot, Eddie Allen, and his test crew of 11 were all killed, together with 19 factory workers and five firemen on the ground.

PRODUCTION

The B-29 was so important to the war effort that urgent improvements were made to the R-3350 to permit production to continue, not only at Boeing's but also by Martin at Omaha, Nebraska, and by Bell at Marietta, Georgia. Although the first XB-29 prototypes were built in Plant One, the 14 YB-29 development aircraft and 1,620 production machines were constructed at the Stearman plant in Wichita.

LEFT The flight engineers position in the Superfortress. Here he could control and monitor all the aircraft's systems including the engines.

BELOW The internal details of the largest bomber of the World War II laid bare. The crew positions and the connecting tunnel are shown in the small inset.

The new bomber, which its test pilot, Eddie Allen, first took into the air on September 21, 1942 had so many new and unique features that it was inevitable that problems would occur. The B-29 was the world's heaviest production aircraft with a wing loading far in excess of anything before it. The defensive armament consisted of four turrets, two above and two below the fuselage, each with a pair of half-inch-calibre machine guns. These turrets were remotely computer-controlled by a pair of gunners aft of the wing.

The tail turret—fitted with either two half-inch machine guns or a single 20 mm cannon—was controlled directly by the tail gunner, who had his own pressurized compartment. The remainder of the crew of 10 were in two separate pressurized areas, one in the nose and the other housing the gunners. It was possible to move between these compartments, since a narrow tube linked them over the central, unpressurized, bomb bays.

The B-29 was powered by four Wright R-3350 engines with 18 cylinders arranged in two rows, each engine giving a

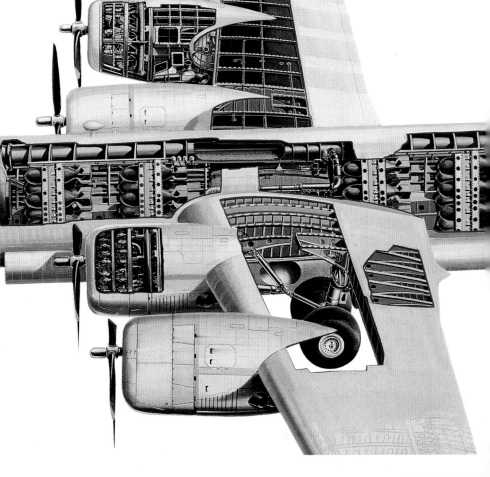

Together with the Martin (204) and Bell (357) a total of 2,181 B-29s were built, before the improved B-29A went into production. This had a new wing center section which increased the wingspan by 12 inches, and a four-gun top-forward turret. All 1,119 A models were built at the new Boeing Renton plant before production finally ceased in May 1946. Together with lightened B-29B models made by Bell Aircraft, a total of 3,627 B-29s were constructed and more than 2,000 were in service at the end of World War II.

IN SERVICE

The first production B-29s were delivered to the Army Air Corps in the fall of 1943, an incredible achievement for a new and very complex aircraft, which had made its first flight only 12 months earlier. Initially operating from bases in India and China, the B-29s started bombing Japan in June 1943. By the summer of 1940, five new airfields had been built on the Marianas Islands, each capable of operating a wing of 180 aircraft. From there Tokyo was attacked for the first time in November 1944. The raids on Japan increased in intensity, especially when, after March 1945, a switch was made to low-level night operations using incendiary rather than high-explosive bombs. The death toll from these attacks was horrific, but it was the dropping of just two bombs that finally ended the war—bombs with which the B-29 will forever be associated.

ABOVE **A B-29 displayed at the Pima Air Museum where the near-desert atmosphere of Tucson, Arizona ensures long-term preservation.**

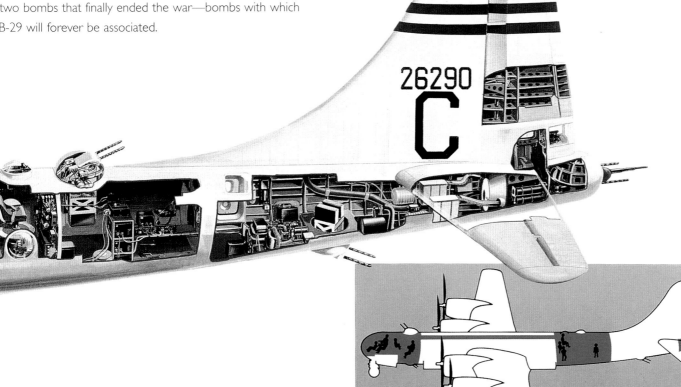

THE ATOM BOMB

The special 509th Composite Group was formed in 1944 with its 393rd Bombardment Squadron (Very Heavy) operating 15 specially modified B-29s. On 6 August 1945 a B-29 piloted by Colonel Paul W. Tibbets and named *Enola Gay*, after the pilot's mother, dropped a 9,700-pound "Little Boy" atomic bomb on its target—Hiroshima. Although the scale of destruction and death was exceeded by the firestorm raids on Tokyo, the fact that just one bomb could cause so much havoc was to change the world overnight. Three days later, a second bomb, code-named "Fat Boy," was dropped on Nagasaki from another B-29 (called *Bockscar*). Japan finally surrendered on August 14, 1945 bringing to a close World War II.

BELOW The nose of the B-29 which changed the history of the world. Named after the pilot's mother, the *Enola Gay* dropped the first atom bomb on Hiroshima.

POSTWAR USE

The B-29 remained the standard bomber of the US Air Force throughout the Korean War and a total of 87 were loaned to the Royal Air Force in 1950 to supplement the aging Avro Lincoln bombers. Renamed the Washington B1, it equipped eight squadrons until the end of 1954.

The Royal Air Force were not the only foreign air force to fly the B-29. The Soviet Air Force did as well. At least three B-29s had made emergency landings in the Soviet Union after bombing Japan. The Tupolev design bureau carefully dismantled them to produce their own production drawings and procedures. At the same time the Shvetsov engine group produced a Wright R-3350 clone under the designation of ASh-73TK, giving 2,300 hp.

Remarkably, the first Tupolev Tu-4 flew for the first time in May 1947 and three production aircraft, together with a passenger version, the Tu-70, were unveiled at the National Air Parade in August 1947.

The Tu-4 had even heavier armament than the B-29, mounting ten 20 mm cannon in five turrets. When production ceased at least 847 Tu-4s had been built and they remained in Soviet service well into the 1960s. A number were also supplied to China, where it is reported some were still in service at the beginning of the 1990s.

Other specialist roles for the B-29 included acting as mothership to the world's first supersonic aircraft, the Bell X-1. Carried semi-recessed on the B-29 bomb bay, the Bell X-1 was dropped at high altitude before igniting its rocket engines. Other B-29s were used for weather reconnaissance, but the most important postwar role for the B-29 was developing in-flight refueling.

LEFT Named Washington 1, 87 B-29s flew with the Royal Air Force for five years from 1950.

IN-FLIGHT REFUELING

The first KB-29M tankers used the British-developed trailing-hose system, but in May 1948 Boeing proposed an alternative method with the primary objective of increasing the refueling rates. This new system used an aerodynamically controlled telescopic pipe (flying boom) which was lowered from the tanker to connect with a socket on the fuselage of the receiving aircraft. Literally the boom operator in the tanker "flew" the nozzle down to the receiver to make a connection. Aerodynamic control was achieved by means of "ruddevators" and extension/retraction of the boom was by hydraulic pressure. The pilot of the receiver had to place his aircraft in a certain position relative to the tanker. To assist him with this task, a series of indicator lights on the tanker indicated right, left, up, down, forward, and aft.

This alternative method was so successful that 116 KB-29s were converted from the standard B-29 during the period 1950–51. It has also, with improvements, remained the primary method of air-to-air refueling for the United States Air Force to this day.

BELOW Using a Boeing-developed refueling system called the "Flying Boom," many B-29s were later converted to in-flight tankers.

MODEL 345-2, B-50 SUPERFORTRESS

An order for 200 Boeing Model 345-2, B-29D aircraft was placed in July 1945, although reduced to 60 after the surrender of Japan. The aircraft was redesignated B-50, partly to obscure the fact that it was a development of an existing model. It also acknowledged that the changes made had produced a 75 percent new design.

Externally the changes were not immediately apparent. For example, a change of material for the wing structure saved 600 pounds in weight but gave a wing 16 percent stronger than that of the B-29. The changes that could be detected included a taller tail and new Pratt & Whitney R-4360 engines, each giving an incredible 3,500 hp—a 59 percent increase in power. These new radial engines had no fewer than 28 cylinders arranged in four rows of seven and a total capacity of 4,360 cubic inches. The R-4360, commonly called the "corncob" engine, since the layout of its cylinders resembled that of an ear of maize, was in effect the ultimate development of the piston engine, both in power output and in complexity.

RIGHT Like its predecessor, B-50 was also converted to an in-flight tanker at the end of its life as a bomber. Here three F-100 Super Sabres are refueled simultaneously.

As a result of the drastic cutbacks in production following the end of the war, the first B-50 did not fly until June 1947. It entered service with the newly formed Strategic Air Command (SAC) shortly afterward, as its first new bomber. Modified later for in-flight refueling, initially using the British hose method, a B-50A "Lucky Lady II" made the first ever nonstop, round-the-world flight on February 26, 1949, being refueled by a relay of six KB-29Ms.

The B-50 continued in production for SAC until 1953, when a total of 371 had been built. Like its B-29 predecessor, as the B-50 approached obsolescence many were converted for weather reconnaissance as WB-50D and as aerial tankers as KB-50J. A number of the former had a pair of General Electric J-47 jet engines fitted outboard of the outer engines to boost the top speed closer to that of the receiving jet-powered aircraft.

After seeing operational service in 1964, refueling jet fighters running low on fuel over Vietnam, the last KB-50s were retired in 1965.

MODEL 367, C-97/KC-97 STRATOFREIGHTER

Using much of the structure of the B-29, the first XC-97 flew in November 1944. The wings, tail undercarriage, and engines were wholly B-29; the fuselage took the form of a double-bubble, the lower section of which had the same diameter as its bomber forebear. The only wholly new structure in the aircraft was the upper lobe of the fuselage with the cargo floor at the intersection of the two bubbles.

BELOW With its flying boom lowered, a KC-97L of the Ohio Air National Guard performs a low flypast for the camera. The two booster jet engines are very apparent.

Ten YC-97 preproduction aircraft were ordered in July 1945, with deliveries starting in October 1947. The later examples were completed with the B-50 tail and R-4360 engines. One of these machines carried more than a million pounds of freight into Berlin on just 27 flights during May 1949 as part of the Berlin Airlift.

Production orders for 50 C-97As followed capable of carrying a 53,000-pound payload or 134 fully equipped troops. Entering service with MATS (Military Air Transport Service) in October 1949, the C-97s were fully employed during the Korean War and also served with SAC, supporting B-50 operations. After a further small order for 14 C-97Cs, all subsequent Stratofreighters built were the KC tanker-transport version. Using the Boeing Flying Boom, 811 KC-97E, F, and G models were delivered between July 1951 and November 1956. Fully committed to Strategic Air Command, each 45-aircraft wing of B-47 Stratojets was supported by 20 KC-97 tankers.

As the KC-135 Stratotankers became more numerous, the KC-97s were transferred to the National Guard Air Units, some designated KC-97L, being fitted with booster J47 jet engines, as had the KB-50 tankers. The final KC-97 tankers were withdrawn from use in 1977.

ABOVE Flown by Agro Air of the Dominican Republic, this former C-97G Stratofreighter was a regular visitor to Miami International Airport in the 1980s.

BELOW The flight deck of the C-97 provided spacious accommodation for its aircrew.

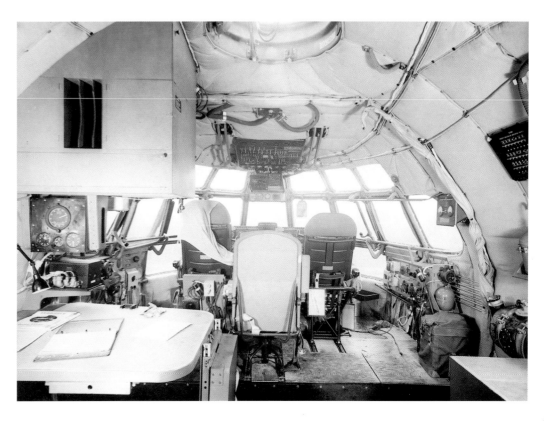

CHAPTER FIVE

JET BOMBERS

LEFT The size, power, and majesty of the mighty B-52 Stratofortress are captured in this dramatic photograph.

ABOVE With the aid of the 33 rockets of its JATO (Jet Assisted Take-Off) pack, a B-47 Stratojet leaps into the air.

This chapter covers just two Boeing designs, the Model 450, B-47 Stratojet and the Model 464, B-52 Stratofortress. The B-47 was Boeing's first jet aircraft; so advanced was it that its configuration continues to be the first choice for designers of multi-engined jet aircraft to this day. Its successor, the B-52, has proved to be so irreplaceable to the United States Air Force that studies have been undertaken to ascertain whether the aircraft can remain in service until around 2040. At the time of writing that sounds incredible, but the B-52 has rewritten history so many times since the first example flew in 1952 that a life of 90 years is not impossible.

MODEL 450, B-47 STRATOJET

When the prototype Stratojet was first revealed to an astounded audience at the Boeing Seattle factory on September 12, 1947, the design employed so many new, revolutionary features that many of the spectators there must have doubted it would even fly. Boeing's first jet bomber, with its engines hung in pods under the highly swept wings, looked so different from its propeller predecessors and all other early jets. However, its configuration was destined, with the sole exception of the Model 727, to be the Boeing design trademark up to the present day.

THE DESIGN

Early design studies for a Boeing jet bomber began in late 1943. But it was access, in May 1945, to German wartime high-speed research that led Boeing's designers to adopt a very thin wing, swept back an amazing 35 degrees. Other contemporary jet designs had all featured the engines buried, either in the fuselage or in the wing roots. Boeing changed all that by hanging their engines in pods from under the wing. The low power of the early jet engines meant that a total of six were required on the aircraft—two in each inner pod and a single engine in the two outboard nacelles.

The thin wing left no room to house a conventional tricycle undercarriage, so yet another radical solution was chosen. A tandem bicycle landing gear was used with balancing outriggers in the inboard engine nacelles. Conceived from the outset to be a nuclear bomber, the complex aircraft was designed to be operated by an unusually small crew of just three. (Boeing's previous bomber, the B-50, had 12 crewmen.) The B-47's pilot and copilot were housed, in tandem, under a fighter-type cockpit canopy and the bombardier/navigator operated from a compartment in the aircraft's nose.

The bomber's high speed at extreme altitudes was expected to make interception by enemy fighters very difficult, if not impossible. Thus the defensive armament was limited to only two tail-mounted guns operated remotely by the copilot or automatically by rear warning radar.

LEFT The first Boeing jet is revealed, the revolutionary XB-47. The roll-out took place on September 12, 1947 at Plant Two in Seattle.

PRODUCTION HISTORY

On the 44th anniversary of the world's first powered flight by the Wright brothers, history was made yet again. It was on December 17, 1947 that Boeing's XB-47 first flew, followed in July 1948 by the second aircraft.

Although the two prototypes were built and flown in Seattle, the factories there were fully committed to existing production of B-50s and KC-97s. A decision was therefore taken that Wichita would be the center for B-47 production.

The initial pilot order under a $30 million contract was for 10 B-47As. These differed from the prototypes in having General Electric J-47 turbojets of 5,200 pounds' thrust, a substantial improvement on the earlier J-35s, which gave only 3,750 pounds of thrust. On the very day the first B-47A flew, Sunday, June 25, 1950, North Korea invaded its southern neighbor, the start of the three-year Korean War. This event meant a massive expansion of production with orders for 399 of the first true production model, the B-47B.

ABOVE **The two pilots cockpits and the instrumentation can be seen in this unusual view.**

BELOW **Details of the construction, the location of all the fuel in the fuselage, and the large size of the single atomic weapon are revealed in this cutaway drawing.**

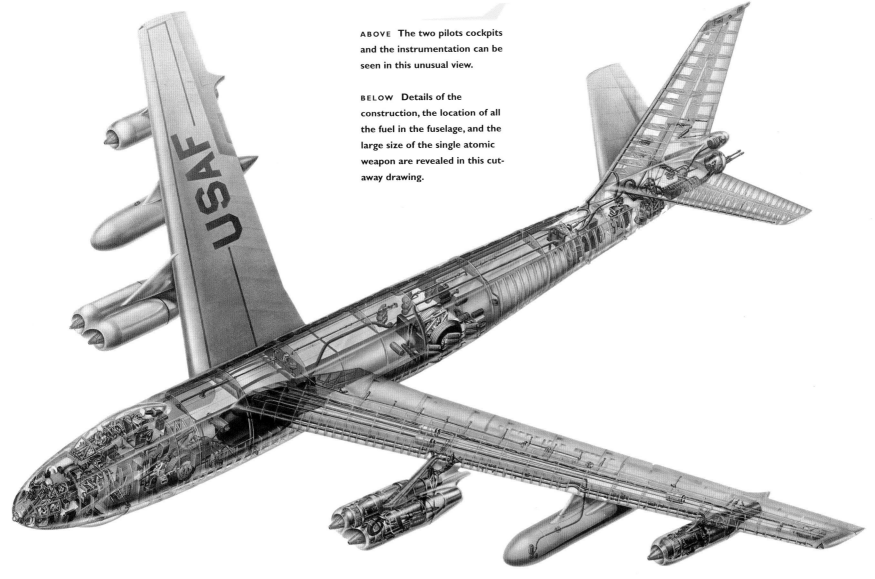

It was considered likely that even Wichita would be incapable of meeting future production demands, so a Boeing-Douglas-Lockheed group was established to build the B-47. Lockheed, at the former Bell plant in Marietta, Georgia, were to build eight B-47B and 385 B-47E models. The third partner, Douglas Aircraft in Tulsa, Oklahoma, constructed 10 B-47B and a further 274 E models.

The B-47E was the major production variant of the design and most of the earlier versions were uprated to the same standard. Engine power was increased to 7,200 pounds by water injection (the very smoky engine trail of most early jet engines was caused by water injection). A jettisonable JATO (Jet-Assisted Take-Off) rocket pack consisting of 33 1,000-pound thrust units could be fitted to improve take-off performance at full load. The twin half-inch tail guns were replaced by two 20 mm cannon and the nose was redesigned to incorporate a standard Boeing socket for in-flight refueling.

There were two experimental XB-47Ds, both modified from B models, the first of which flew in July 1955. They were used as flight test beds for the Curtiss Wright T49 turboprop engines, at the time the most powerful engine of the type. However, their installation in the inboard nacelles of the B-47 aircraft was not a success and helped hasten the decline of the once mighty Wright Company.

A more successful production version of the B-47 was the RB-47E strategic photo-reconnaissance, which featured a lengthened nose in which the bombardier became a photographer/navigator. Wichita built 240 of this version, which first flew in August 1953. A later reconnaissance version was the RB-47H, 32 of which were built by Boeing for the detection and location of surface radar stations.

When production of new aircraft ceased in February 1957, a total of 2,032 B-47s had been built, 1,373 by Boeing Wichita.

ABOVE **The important second XB-47 guards the entrance to Chanute Air Force Base, Illinois.**

OPERATIONAL HISTORY

The first unit in Strategic Air Command (SAC) to receive the B-47 was the renowned 306th Bomb Wing. As the 306th Bomb Group, during World War II, it had flown the Boeing B-17 Flying Fortress from England as part of the Mighty Eighth Air Force. The famous movie *Twelve O'Clock High* was based on the wartime exploits of the 306th. Deliveries of the B-47B began in October 1951 and soon the 306th had their full complement of 45 aircraft.

Much of the training carried out by the B-47 crews was for their primary role of dropping nuclear weapons from high altitude. The early bombs were large but, as smaller weapons became available and high altitude defenses grew stronger, the "lob-bombing" technique was evolved. This procedure made use of the fighter-like agility of the B-47, albeit with factory-reinforced wings. At high speed, close to ground level, the bomber would pull up into a half-loop, releasing the bomb as the aircraft climbed. As the bomb continued on its trajectory toward the target, the bomber rolled out at the top of the loop to dive safely away from the resulting explosion.

This spectacular technique was first publicly demonstrated in May 1957—without releasing a bomb, of course! Also in 1957, B-47 numbers in SAC reached a peak with approximately 1,800 planes in service. The aircraft, both in numbers and capabilities, totally dominated the United States nuclear deterrent force for 10 years from 1953. Earlier aircraft like the Boeing B-29/B-50 and the Convair B-36 were being phased out of service during the mid to late 1950s. The mighty B-52, although entering service in 1955, took until 1960 to reach a total of 500 available to SAC.

With the supersonic Convair B-58 Hustler then entering service and growing numbers of strategic Intercontinental Ballistic Missiles (ICBMs), including Boeing's Minuteman missiles, SAC's need for the B-47 diminished rapidly. In 1966 the last Stratojet was retired from front-line service. Although it was to be overshadowed by its bigger, younger brother, the B-47 performed a vital role during probably the most crucial period of the Cold War. Its innovative technological features are still to be seen at every airport worldwide.

STRATEGIC AIR COMMAND (SAC)

Formed in 1946 with its motto "Peace is our Profession," SAC was America's nuclear deterrent force for nearly 44 years of the Cold War. Together with land-based and submarine-launched missiles, SAC's aircraft provided the means of attacking the cities and other strategic targets in the former Soviet Union. In a policy called "Mutually Assured Destruction" (with its appropriate acronym, MAD), the two superpowers continually enlarged their nuclear forces, seeking to achieve an overwhelming superiority. The policy, on each side, was to be able to survive an initial attack by their opponent and then launch a devastating nuclear reply.

Bomber and refueling tanker aircraft of Strategic Air Command were based at airfields throughout the United States, and also in Britain, Morocco, Spain, and in the Pacific. One-third of the bomber force were maintained on permanent ground alert, fully armed with nuclear weapons, with the crews ready for immediate take-off. A further force were Airborne-Alert.

In rotation, with air-to-air refueling, nuclear-armed aircraft were permanently in the air, invulnerable to a surprise attack on their bases. During periods of international tension—for example, during the 1962 Cuba crisis—SAC was on full 24-hour alert with its aircraft dispersed worldwide.

With the ending of the Cold War, its duty done, Strategic Air Command was de-activated in 1992. Its aircraft, together with those of the former Tactical Air Command, were brought together in June 1997 into the new Air Combat Command.

MODEL 464, B-52 STRATOFORTRESS

The B-47 was an incredible technological breakthrough but to the commander of Strategic Air Command it was never big enough. He also hated the tandem position of the pilot and copilot. General Curtiss E. Le May was a heavy-bomber man. Involved in the very first Air Corps use of the B-17, moving through commands of B-17 and B-29 Groups and their Divisions, he became the SAC commander in 1948. For nine of the most critical years of the Cold War he was to have a crucial influence on US policy.

Because it could carry only a single atom bomb, the B-47 was classified as a medium bomber. Le May wanted something much bigger, capable of carrying a 10,000-pound bomb load for at least 3,500 miles, and returning.

THE DESIGN

In October 1948, Boeing submitted a straight-winged, six-turboprop-powered design to the US Air Force at Wright Field, Ohio, which, prompted by Le May, rejected it. A six-man Boeing team, ensconced in their Dayton hotel rooms, over the following weekend totally redesigned the proposal. In a story that has a strong flavor of Hollywood, the team returned to Wright Field on the Monday morning with a design for an eight-engined, swept-wing bomber plus a balsa-wood model! This was accepted and led to an order for two prototypes, designated XB-52 and YB-52.

THE PROTOTYPES

In November 1951, the first XB-52 was moved out of Plant Two under security wraps, which did little to conceal its size and appearance. Ground tests, including taxiing, were protracted and the aircraft returned to the factory for further work to be completed. Thus it was the YB-52 that first flew in April 1952. This historic machine is now preserved at the Air Force Museum at Wright Patterson Air Force Base, Dayton, Ohio, the place where the design was born.

Both prototypes looked very much like a scaled-up B-47, even down to the tandem arrangement for the pilot and copilot under a fighter-type bubble canopy. The increased complexity of the B-52 necessitated a five-man rather than the three-man crew of the B-47. However, this compared very favorably with SAC's then heavy bomber, the gigantic Convair B-36 Peacemaker, which required a crew of 22. Convair also produced a jet version of the B-36, the eight-engined YB-60. When this monster aircraft flew in April 1952, it was found to be over 100 m.p.h. slower than the B-52. Boeing's mastery of the big bomber was unchallenged.

BELOW The YB-52 first flew on April 15, 1952. This historic aircraft is now preserved in the USAF Museum.

LEFT Eight of everything! Eight engine throttle levers and eight sets of engine instruments dominate this photograph of the flight deck of a **B-52D.**

The B-52 had its share of unique features, although fewer than its smaller brother. Perhaps the most interesting was the ability of the four main undercarriage assemblies to swivel at an angle to the fuselage alignment. This resulted in a very complex main undercarriage but enabled the aircraft to land in a severe crosswind with the wheels aligned along the runway when the rest of the aircraft was facing into the wind. Pilots initially found this very disconcerting but grew to like the ease in which crosswind landings could be achieved.

As with the B-47, the only defensive armament was a tail turret, initially having four half-inch machine guns, which could be fired either manually by a gunner or automatically by tail warning radar. The eight Pratt & Whitney J-57 engines mounted on the 35-degree swept wing were in four pairs and each produced 8,700 pounds of thrust. The two prototypes weighed 390,000 pounds fully loaded and had a maximum speed of 556 m.p.h. at high altitude.

General Le May liked most of what he saw of the new bomber but definitely not the pilots' seating arrangements. Despite the potential aerodynamic advantages of tandem seating, he insisted that his pilots sit side by side—so the design was changed.

BELOW The B-52A continues its flight test program after the original pilots tandem seating (as in the B-47) was replaced by side-by-side seats.

ABOVE The sting in the tail of a B-52G. In this version the four 0.50 inch guns were fired automatically or controlled remotely by a gunner in the aircraft's nose.

INTO SERVICE

Initially just 13 B-52As were ordered in February 1951 since a fly-off was envisaged between it and the Convair YB-60 for a large production order. As we have seen, the Convair, when it flew, posed no threat to the B-52. Thus when the first B-52A flew in August 1954 the YB-60 had already been eliminated, so only three A-model B-52s were built. All three were used for research-and-development work. Perhaps the most dramatic was the one that was converted, in 1959, to carry the North American X-15 rocket-powered research aircraft. Dropped from the B-52, the X-15 was to reach speeds in excess of 4,500 m.p.h.

The true-production B-52B and RB-52B were initially the 10 unwanted B-52As fitted with improved engines, plus a further 40 new-build aircraft. The first B model was delivered to SAC in June 1955 for the 93rd Heavy Bombardment Wing at Castle Air Force Base, California. History was made between January 16 and 18, 1957 when three of the 93rd's aircraft flew nonstop around the world in just 45 hours, 19 minutes. The B-52s were refueled three times enroute by Boeing KC-97 tankers.

Another first was that the three tail gunners became the first men to fly round the world backwards. The B-52B also dropped the first hydrogen bomb during a test over Bikini Atoll on May 21, 1956. Another B-52B joined forces with its A-model sister, being converted to NB-52B to join the X-15 program.

IMPROVED MODELS

A steady stream of improved versions of the B-52 came from the Boeing factories during the 1950s with ever more powerful engines and increased maximum weights, until the B-52F flew in May 1958. This featured the 13,750-pound-thrust Pratt & Whitney J-57P and it was the last model of the B-52 to be jointly built in both Seattle and Wichita.

The B-52G, built wholly in Wichita, had significant technical changes and for the first time a visual recognition feature to distinguish it from its predecessors. The 48-foot-high fin of the B-52 was, in the G, reduced to 40 feet 8 inches with increased chord. Fuel capacity was significantly increased both by integral tanks in the wing and enlarged 700-gallon tanks outboard of the outrigger wheels. The tail guns became remotely operated, the tail gunner leaving his isolated position in the tail to join the electronic-countermeasures operator in the front compartment below the two pilots.

ABOVE A B-52 Stratofortress displays exceptional maneuvrability for such a large aircraft.

LEFT The boom operator at the tail of a Boeing KC-135 tanker gets a close-up view of a B-52.

Also in this area, but facing forward, sat the bombardier and radar navigator, making up the crew of six. The non-refueled range of the G model was demonstrated in December 1960 when a 5th Bombardment Wing aircraft flew 10,000 miles in 19 hours 45 minutes—over 3,500 miles further than the longest flight by a B-52D.

Further increases in range were made possible in the B-52H, which had the more economical 16,000-pound-thrust Pratt & Whitney TF-33 turbofans fitted. Also, the old half-inch machine guns were replaced by a multibarrel, quick-firing Gatling gun.

Flying from Okinawa to Spain in January 1962, a B-52H set a new nonrefueled distance record of 12,519 miles. The H model was the final version of the B-52, and the delivery of the last aircraft in October 1962 brought to an end the production of the 744 aircraft. But the end of production was just the beginning for the B-52.

THE B-52 AND VIETNAM

Although designed as a high-altitude nuclear bomber, the B-52 went to war dropping conventional high-explosive bombs during the Vietnam War. The use of the B-52 started in June 1965 when two wings of the B-52F aircraft were sent to the island of Guam in the Pacific. With refueling by Boeing KC-135 tankers, a typical round-trip bombing mission took over 13 hours.

At the end of 1965 a decision was taken to modify the whole B-52D fleet to accommodate an increased load of conventional, so-called "iron bombs." The "big-belly" B-52s (as they became known) were capable of carrying up to 84 500-pound bombs or 42 750-pound bombs in the bomb bay plus another 24 750-pounders under the wings. This added up to a maximum bomb load of 60,000 pounds, three times the standard B-52 conventional bomb load—also, incidentally, the equivalent of the bomb load of eight Boeing B-17Gs. The

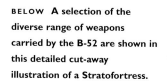

BELOW A selection of the diverse range of weapons carried by the B-52 are shown in this detailed cut-away illustration of a Stratofortress.

modified B-52Ds became operational over Vietnam in 1966, replacing the B-52Fs.

Initially the B-52 was used as a tactical bomber, albeit bombing from 30,000 feet or above, using radar to find the targets, which were often Vietcong troop concentrations. The accuracy of these attacks, from aircraft that were virtually invisible, was totally demoralizing but did little to stem the Vietcong advance. The strategic use of the B-52 began in 1966 with the bombing of North Vietnam. It was over the city of Hanoi on December 26, 1972 that the largest concentration of B-52s was deployed—a total of 117 aircraft. Generally about 200 B-52s were employed at any one time, based in both Guam and Thailand.

The main opposition to the B-52 was the Soviet-built SA-2 surface-to-air missiles (SAMs) with the NATO code name "Guideline." These long (35-foot) missiles had a range of 28 miles and an effective ceiling of 82,000 feet. With a maximum speed of Mach 2.5 (two and a half times the speed of sound), these missiles posed a formidable threat to the effectiveness of the B-52. Usually they were detected on radar and then, owing to their size, visually, when effective evasive action could be taken. However, 17 B-52s were lost to enemy action and many other aircraft managed to return to base with varying degrees of damage.

In the eight years in which the B-52 was deployed over Vietnam, a total of 126,615 sorties were flown.

THE 1991 GULF WAR

The B-52's unique value is, as always, as a very long-range carrier of weapons of all descriptions. Throughout its 43-year operational history, the B-52 has carried an increasingly sophisticated range of missiles and bombs. Today these are primarily of the cruise missile variety. During the Gulf War of 1991, the primary weapon was the AGM-86C Conventional Air-Launched Cruise Missile (CALCM). Their first use was within 90 minutes of the start of Operation Desert Storm.

In those opening minutes, two groups of aircraft were attacking Iraq. The first were 10 F-117 stealth fighters, the latest aircraft in the US Air Force inventory; the others were seven B-52Gs, which had left Barksdale Air Force Base, Louisiana, almost 12 hours before H hour (timed for 3 am, Baghdad time, January 17, 1991). The seven aircraft were part of the 2nd Bombardment Wing, one of seven such wings in SAC's Eighth Air Force (successor to the wartime Mighty Eighth) with its HQ also at Barksdale.

In a mission that was not revealed until exactly a year later, the seven B-52s undertook the longest air-combat mission in history. (The previous record had been held by an RAF Vulcan during the 1982 Falklands War.)

The bombers were each refueled four times during their 14,000-mile, 35-hour round trip before returning to the Barksdale base. A total of 31 CALCMs were launched from outside Iraq's air defenses to attack power and communications stations. The success of this incredible mission was a tribute to the sophistication of the missiles, the endurance of the crews in their cramped quarters, and the unique capabilities of the B-52.

The very long-distance attack was a one-off, but 73 B-52s were committed to the conflict in the Gulf. Based in Saudi Arabia, on Diego Garcia, and in England and Spain, the B-52s undertook 1,624 missions to deliver 72,000 bombs (38 percent of the total dropped by the USAF).

Today there are 94 surviving B-52Hs left in service. They are capable of carrying up to eight AGM-86B Air-Launched Cruise Missiles (ALCM) from a rotary launcher in the bomb bay, plus 12 more missiles under the wings. The Advanced Cruise Missile (ACM) is more stealthy than its predecessor but is too large to fit in the bomb-bay launcher, so 12 are carried under the B-52's wings. Of course, the B-52 can still carry free-fall nuclear weapons.

For the future, Boeing has submitted a proposal to replace the eight engines with four Rolls-Royce RB211-535s. These proven, highly economical, civil power plants would, Boeing estimates, save about $6 billion in operational and support costs over the next 25 years. The proposal has yet to receive the go-ahead but, whatever the outcome, the B-52 is scheduled to be an important part of the USAF for many years to come.

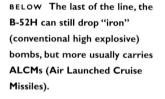

BELOW The last of the line, the B-52H can still drop "iron" (conventional high explosive) bombs, but more usually carries ALCMs (Air Launched Cruise Missiles).

ABOVE A B-52H trails its braking parachute to reduce the length of the landing run.

LEFT The 185 feet wingspan and outrigger landing gear are emphasized in this photograph.

RIGHT The end of the road for redundant B-52Ds. In the Aerospace Maintenance and Regeneration Center (AMARC), Davis Monthan AFB, Arizona, cold war warriors await the scrapheap.

CHAPTER SIX

FIRST-GENERATION JET TRANSPORTS

LEFT Originally built as a Boeing 707 for American Airlines but converted to an E-8A under the J-STARS (Joint Surveillance and Target Attack Radar System) program, this aircraft operated in the 1991 Gulf War and over Bosnia.

ABOVE Capable of carrying between 126 and 149 passengers, the first Next Generation 737–700 is photographed on an early test flight.

In the early years after World War II, Boeing's reputation was based on its wartime manufacture of military aircraft, despite moderate sales of the Model 377 Stratocruiser (see Chapter Three). It was, however, the remarkable B-47 Stratojet that was to inspire the transport revolution that made the name of Boeing synonymous with jet airliners.

Boeing was not the first to design and build a jet transport. That honor went to the British de Havilland company, whose DH106 Comet first flew in July 1949 and entered service in May 1952. The little-known phenomenon of metal fatigue was to prove the Comet's undoing. After two aircraft had disintegrated at high altitude, the aircraft was grounded in 1954 for a compete redesign. While the Comet was apparently sweeping all before it, Boeing had not been idle. The then president of the company, William Allen—who was to make his mark indelibly, not only on Boeing but on the whole of the aerospace industry —was convinced that a Boeing jet transport should be built.

Design studies based on the Model 367, then entering service with the US Air Force as the C-97 Stratofreighter (see Chapter Four), progressed through numerous concepts until number 80 was reached. The Model 367-80 bore no resemblance to the original 367 design, but it was under this designation that the aircraft that was to become the world-famous Boeing 707 was born.

MODEL 367-80

The company had had a dual function in mind for its new design from the outset, as a civilian airliner and as a military tanker-transport. In-flight refueling of the jet Boeing B-47 by the propeller-powered KC-97 had proved possible. But it required the bomber not only to slow down to near stalling speed but also to fly at lower altitudes in order to take on fuel. A jet-powered tanker would have obvious substantial operational advantages, but the company was unable to convince the US Air Force that its paper concept was viable.

Despite this potential dual role, the decision in May 1952 to build the first Model 367-80 was a major financial gamble by Boeing, investing no less than $16 million (said then to be half the company's total assets). However, William Allen and his board of directors were convinced that the design was so advanced that it would revolutionize world travel.

So it proved, but not without a nerve-racking struggle.

The airplane, which was unveiled for the first time on May 14, 1954, combined the 35-degree swept-back wing of its jet-bomber predecessors, married to a fuselage having the same vertical double-bubble concept of the C-97 but without the noticeable joint line. The fuselage width of 132 inches remained the same. It must be remembered that the Model 367-80 was purely an experimental prototype built to demonstrate the practicality of the design. It therefore had few windows or internal fittings.

In the hands of Boeing's chief test pilot, "Tex" Johnson, the new aircraft flew for the first time on July 15, 1954. Despite insurance to the value of $15 million, the future of the Boeing Company rested on the success of this one aircraft. Johnson was soon very confident about the new airplane, such that he later barrel-rolled the aircraft over Lake Washington during a demonstration for the International Air Transport Association (IATA), much to the consternation of the company president, William Allen.

The testing and evaluation of the Dash 80, as it became universally known, divided into two paths: the development of the tanker-transport for the Air Force, to be called the KC-135, and the commercial version under the designation of Model 707. A description of these designs follows. The Dash 80 continued to serve the company as a development machine for the Boeing 727 and other projects until its retirement in 1972. It was then presented to the National Air and Space Museum of the Smithsonian Institution, who have designated it as one of the 12 most significant aircraft of all time.

MODEL 707

Efforts by the Boeing sales team to interest the world's airlines in their new product in the form of the 367-80 were met with a very lukewarm reception. Despite increasing the cabin width by 12 inches to meet the US Air Force requirements for the KC-135, the cabin was still felt to be too small. The Douglas Aircraft Company was offering a larger, more powerful design, the DC-8, which, although still a paper concept, was backed by the company's reputation as the world's leading transport manufacturer. It looked as if history was about to repeat itself, as in the 1930s, when Boeing's lead with the revolutionary Model 247 was lost to the larger Douglas DC-1, DC-2, and the renowned DC-3.

Boeing targeted the leading American airline, Pan American World Airlines—universally known as Pan-Am—who had traditionally bought Boeing, having introduced both the Model 307 and Model 314 into service. Competition for that first order was very fierce, both on price and on specification. Finally, on October 13, 1955, a nail-biting 14 months after the Dash 80 first flew, Pan Am ordered 20 707-100s with a cabin width increased by yet a further four inches to permit six-abreast seating, matching the DC-8. However, Pan Am still felt that the Douglas was potentially a better aircraft and—simultaneously—ordered

25 DC-8s. Further orders for the DC-8 convinced Boeing that they had to improve the 707, and they began to offer a fuselage 10 feet longer and more powerful engines.

At the end of 1955, orders for the 707 totaled 73, and, while Douglas was still ahead with 98 on order, thereafter the 707 led the way.

ABOVE The growing outcry against jet noise during the late 1950s is reflected in this view of a Pan American 707 fitted with noise reduction exhaust nozzles.

BELOW A busy production line of 707s as Boeing increase the output to meet the worldwide demand from the airlines and passengers.

BELOW The livery of American Airlines seen here was typical of the late 1950s.

BELOW The 707 had a flight-deck crew of four; two pilots, a navigator on the left, and a flight engineer to the right.

INTO SERVICE

The 707 entered service with Pan Am on October 26, 1958. Although designed primarily for the transcontinental route across America, for reasons of prestige, the first passengers were carried on the New York—Paris route. However, the 707 was not the first jet to carry fare-paying passengers across the Atlantic: that honor had been achieved just three weeks earlier by its old, smaller rival, the de Havilland Comet—totally redesigned in its Mark 4 version and operated by the British Overseas Airways Corporation (BOAC).

Despite the publicity of the transatlantic service, it was across America that the 707 made its greatest impact. Carrying up to 179 passengers for just over 3,900 miles, it halved the flying time on every route it operated, immediately making its piston-engined Douglas and Lockheed predecessors obsolete.

LONG RANGE 707

The true long-range 707 was the Boeing 707-320 Intercontinental with an increased wingspan of 12 feet plus a fuselage stretched by eight feet, giving the capability of carrying nearly 200 passengers for almost 4,800 miles. Again it was Pan Am who first put this version into service on the Pacific routes in August 1959.

Although BOAC operated the Comet 4 worldwide it was not competitive with the 707, and the British carrier urgently needed to buy the American product. This became politically possible when Rolls-Royce Conway bypass engines became an optional replacement for the original Pratt & Whitney JT4 turbojets. This version became the 707-400 series. Offering as it did much-improved fuel economy, increased range, and reduced take-off noise, it was a popular version of the design.

Pratt & Whitney responded by fitting a fan to the front of its earlier JT3C turbojet, giving a 41 percent increase in power and giving rise to the name "turbofan" for this version of jet engine. The new JT3D became the standard engine for all future 707s and DC-8s. The concept of a front fan is now universal for all commercial jet engines.

BOEING MODEL 720

Even before the 707 Intercontinental entered service, a version of the 707 optimized for short to medium routes and shorter runways was under development. Initially called the 707-020, it eventually became the 720.

Visually indistinguishable from the 707, the 720 was much lighter, having a fuselage nine feet shorter than the standard 707-100 and a much-revised wing. Sixty-five of the initial version

were built and when the turbofan became available a further 89 720B models were delivered to their airline customers. Production of the 707/720 and its derivatives ceased in 1991 after a total of 1,010 had been built. Its rival, the DC-8, reached just over half that total at 556, underlining the eventual superiority of the Boeing product.

When statistics were last calculated at the end of 1997, the Boeing 707/720 fleet had accumulated almost 36½ million flying hours and made nearly 14 million landings. One aircraft, then in service with Beta Cargo of Brazil, had flown over 92,000 hours since delivery to Lufthansa in 1967. That total is the equivalent to over 10½ years of continuous flying! Not bad for an aircraft initially given a design flying life of just 30,000 hours. By improved inspection and maintenance procedures, this design life has constantly been extended.

Of the 100 or so 707/720s still in service at the end of 1998, almost all were carrying cargo rather than passengers. Owing to increasing restrictions on noise and exhaust emissions, the aircraft remaining in service are now either being re-engined or having noise-reducing "hushkits" fitted. However, it can be safely predicted that the last commercial use of the aircraft, which made possible Boeing's world dominance of the airliner market, will be many years into the twenty-first century.

BELOW Two Boeing aircraft operated by Lufthansa; a long range 707 Intercontinental in the foreground with the smaller, short to medium range Model 720 behind. Note the noise suppressors on the Intercontinental.

RIGHT **The boom operator's station on the Boeing KC-135 tanker. Lying prone, the operator rests his chest on the padded support (seen on the left) to "fly" the boom down to the receiving aircraft.**

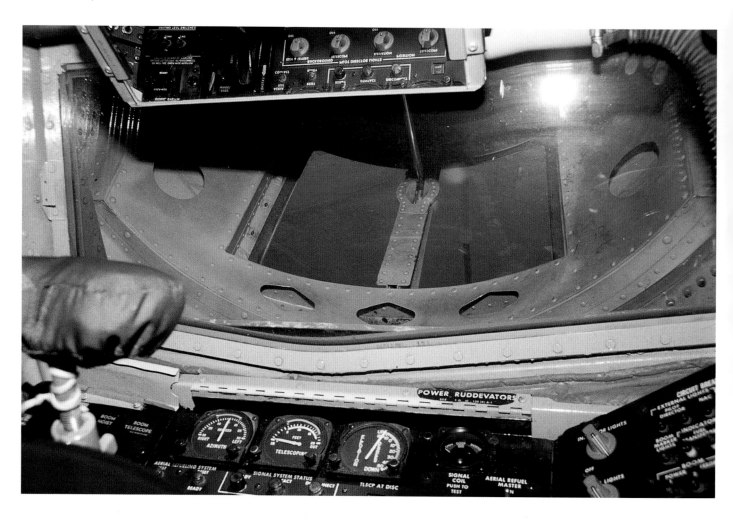

THE MILITARY 707

As we have already seen, Boeing envisaged a military role for the Model 367-80 from the very beginning. The prototype was soon flying with a Boeing "flying boom" refueling unit installed for demonstration purposes. The gamble of the privately funded prototype paid off in September 1954 with an initial order for 29 KC-135A jet tanker-transports for the US Air Force. The model number 707 had been reserved for the commercial version of the 367-80. Model number 717 was therefore chosen for the KC-135. (In view of the bitter competition with Douglas, it is ironic that this model number is now being applied to the design originally launched in October 1995 as the McDonnell Douglas MD-95. This situation has come about by the merging of McDonnell Douglas with Boeing in August 1997.)

In this section, therefore, we shall be looking at two slightly different military 707 aircraft and their derivatives: the original model 717 version with its 144-inch-wide fuselage, and those derived from the commercial 707 with an additional four inches of fuselage width.

BELOW **A re-engined KC-135R is escorted by four General Dynamics F-111 bombers in an airshow flypast.**

THE MODEL 717, KC-135 STRATOTANKER

The impact of this new tanker was emphasized at the formal roll-out in July 1956. The event was orchestrated so that the last of the Model 717's propeller predecessors, the KC-97, preceded it onto the Renton factory apron. Carrying the name *City of Renton* beneath the cockpit, the first KC-135A took to the air on August 31, 1956 to embark on a series of development, test, and evaluation programs.

Powered by four Pratt & Whitney J57 turbojets, each of 13,750-pounds' thrust, the new tanker was an impressive sight. It was capable of carrying a total of 31,200 gallons in its fuselage and wing tanks, and its load was normally dispensed via the standard flying boom but could have an adapter fitted to use the British probe and drogue system. The tanker trailed a flexible hose with a cone at the end into which the receiving aircraft inserted a probe to make a connection. According to USAF figures, the initial cost of a KC-135 when it entered service in June 1957 was $3,670,000. Currently, the KC-135 is valued by the air force at over $52 million each!

ABOVE The KC-135 boom operators view of another Boeing aircraft, the incomparable B-52.

RIGHT A double roll-out ceremony took place on the Renton tarmac on 18 July 1956 as the last KC-97 introduced its jet replacement, the KC-135 Stratotanker.

RIGHT In the mid-1980s, a KC-135A approaches to land at RAF Mildenhall, Suffolk, England, the main European base for USAF tanker aircraft.

LEFT One of the more unusual uses of the ubiquitous 135, the sixth aircraft was converted in 1977 to a NKC-135A as an Airborne Laser Laboratory, the forerunner of the StarWars program of the 1990s.

BELOW The larger diameter cowlings of the more economical **CFM56** turbofan engines are an easy recognition feature of the **KC-135R** variant.

PRODUCTION AND VARIANTS

When the last aircraft was delivered in January 1965, a total of 820 Model 717s had been built, the majority (732) being delivered as KC-135As. A further 45 were built as pure transports under the C-135 designation but the remainder were adapted to serve an increasingly varied range of specialist duties. These included the EC-135C as airborne command posts; the RC-135A, used for photo-mapping; and the RC-135C, used for strategic reconnaissance. Over the years, this range of duties grew until, at the latest count, there have been over 30 different variants of the 135, many with increasingly bizarre protrusions from the fuselage. Inevitably for an aircraft that has been in service for over 40 years, many upgrades and improvements have been made during that time. Perhaps the most obvious, at least externally, has been to the engines.

An interim improvement was the replacement of the J57 turbojet with a Pratt & Whitney TF33 turbofan, to produce the C-135B, but the most significant change was the fitting of the General Electric/SNECMA CFM56 high-bypass-ratio turbofans. These very large-diameter engines are an instant recognition feature of the KC-135R. Giving a thrust of over 22,000 pounds each, and being much quieter and fuel-efficient, they transformed the performance of the KC 135. An increase of 15 percent in payload/range and the ability to deliver 20 percent more fuel have meant that, to date, nearly 450 of the original KC-135s have been converted.

The value of the KC-135 can best be judged by the statistics it achieved during the 1990–91 Gulf crisis and war. The number of aircraft was built up from an initial 32 to an amazing 256, based throughout Europe and the Middle East. In the build-up period (Operation Desert Shield) the KC-135 undertook nearly 5,000 sorties with over 19,000 flying hours to deliver 6.8 million gallons to more than 14,000 receiving aircraft. Even these impressive statistics were exceeded during Desert Storm. Over 15,000 sorties delivered fuel to nearly 46,000 receivers during 60,000 hours of flying. An incredible 132 million gallons of fuel delivered in the air in just six weeks.

No wonder that final retirement for the KC-135 is not envisaged before 2032, when each aircraft will be more than 70 years old.

MODEL 707—MILITARY VARIANTS

Of the many versions of the 707 that have either been bought new for military use or converted from former civil airliners perhaps the most famous are the VIP transports under the designation of the VC-137

The first of an initial three VC-137s flew in 1959 but the order in 1961 of two special 707s under designation of VC-137C were for the specific use of President John F. Kennedy. The first of these, serial number 26000, is always referred to as Air Force One, but in practice any VIP aircraft when carrying the President uses that call sign.

The VC-137 continued to serve as VIP aircraft until 1990 before being replaced by the VC-25 version of the Boeing 747. The original 26000 is now preserved in the US Air Force Museum at Wright-Patterson Air Force Base in Dayton, Ohio.

BELOW The most famous version of the **707/135 family, the** Presidential **VC-137C lands for** the last time at **Wright-Patterson Air Force Base for** preservation by the USAF Museum.

THE AWACS

If the VC-137 is the most famous, the most easily recognizable version of the 707 is the AWACS (Airborne Warning and Control System). Equipped with a large rotating radar mounted above the fuselage, the AWACS aircraft has a 360-degree view of the horizon and at its operating height can "see" more than 200 miles. Its role is to detect and track airborne and sea-surface targets, directing defending or offensive aircraft to intercept the target. Under the military designation of E-3 Sentry, the first of 34 aircraft for the United States Air Force was delivered in March 1977. A further 18 E-3s were acquired by the North Atlantic Treaty Organization (NATO) with the deliveries beginning early in 1982. Unusually these aircraft carry USAF serial numbers but are registered as civil airplanes in Luxembourg.

Further deliveries were made to Saudi Arabia, France, and the United Kingdom. The seven British Sentry AEW Is replaced the venerable Avro Shackleton with the No.8 Squadron, RAF, as the UK's Airborne Early Warning unit. With the delivery of the RAF aircraft, the 707 production line finally closed in May 1991. Today in Britain, Marshall Aerospace of Cambridge share a sister design authority for the RAF Sentry with Boeing and carried out the first major servicing of the fleet over a two-year period during 1997–98. From the original Model 367-80 of 1954, a total of 1,830 aircraft of the 707/717/720 family were built in a production run that lasted over 35 years.

It marked a truly satisfactory outcome of the original Boeing gamble to build the Dash 80 prototype plane and firmly established the company as the world's leading commercial aircraft manufacturer.

TOP This Royal Air Force Boeing E-3D Sentry AEW I carries the squadron markings of number 8 Squadron, which provides the airborne early warning defense of the UK.

ABOVE A NATO operated AWACS takes off from the USAF base at RAF Mildenhall, England.

MODEL 727

The success of the Boeing 707, with its great passenger appeal of speed combined with smooth, vibration-free flight above the weather, created a demand for the jet-powered aircraft on the shorter routes for which even the 720 was not designed. The turboprop aircraft, like the Vickers Viscount and Lockheed Electra, met some of these needs but not that of speed. Passengers wanted performance.

Boeing recognized this demand and in 1956 initiated studies into the type of jet transport that could fulfill the apparent conflicting requirement of speed, with the ability to operate from short runways at small airports with few facilities. This period was a difficult time for the Boeing Company. The development of the 707/720 was proving to be very expensive, especially since the different fuselage widths of the 707 and KC-135 necessitated two separate production lines and manufacturing jigs. The need to simultaneously develop the long-range intercontinental version and the original 707-120, although ensuring the success of the 707, pushed Boeing's balance sheet even further into the red. A willingness to tailor the aircraft to the needs of the customer, in particular the fuselage length, helped win orders and generate future goodwill, but did little to reduce the company's financial overspend. It would be many years before sales of these aircraft repaid their development costs and then started to make profits.

By 1958 the company's finances were little better but the board of directors gave a conditional go-ahead to the new project. However, unlike with the 707, there could be no building first and then the getting of orders: the 727 would be built only when 100 firm orders had been secured.

THE DESIGN

The airplane that the Boeing salesmen were trying to sell looked very different from the 707 but in fact had a lot of common structure. The fuselage width was the same, using the identical upper fuselage with a similar flight deck. It was with the wing and particularly the mounting of the engines where the 727 totally departed from what had become the standard configuration for all Boeing jet aircraft. The 727 had its three engines all at the tail!

The tail mounting of engines on airliners had been pioneered by the French Sud Aviation Company with their twin-engined Caravelle in 1955. Boeing's old British rival, the de Havilland Company, was about to receive an order for a three-engined aircraft, which visually looked identical to the 727 design. Sadly for de Havilland and the Hawker Siddeley Group, into which de Havilland later merged, the first design was judged

ABOVE An unusual visitor to Heathrow in the spring of 1980 was this Mexican Air Force Boeing 727.

BELOW The first Boeing 727 displays some of its special features; integral ventral airstairs, T tail and three engines, all fitted with thrust reversers for a short landing run.

to be too large for British European Airways. This delay put the Trident behind the 727 and made it too small for most airline customers. The Trident never matched the success of its American rival.

The tail mounting of engines had certain advantages over the wing position:

● There is little or no risk of damage to the engines from ingesting debris from the runway

● Noise levels in the cabin, especially on take-off, are much reduced

● The grouping of engines also permit the mixing of bypass air with the exhaust to reduce air velocity and therefore noise levels

● The handling of the aircraft with an engine out of action is much easier and safer

● The wing, being unrestricted by engines, is more efficient and the design of special devices to further increase efficiency is simpler

BELOW A Pan American 727 demonstrates the full array of wing-high lift devices which made it possible for the aircraft to use small, high altitude airports.

This last factor was perhaps the most critical since the 727 was being designed with very complex flaps which could extend both from the front and the rear of the wing. These high-lift devices would enable the 727 to operate from runways as short as 5,000 feet, which hitherto had been accessible only to propeller-driven aircraft.

Inevitably, there were disadvantages to the configuration. In particular, the concentration of weight at the rear gave rise to difficulty in keeping the balance with varying passenger and fuel loads. The T position of the tail also had an inherent potential danger called "the deep stall." In this, an aircraft in a high nose-up attitude could find that turbulence from its wings prevented the tail plane (horizontal stabilizer) from functioning. The aircraft would just fall from the sky—this, in fact, happened to a prototype of the British Aircraft Corporation BAC One-Eleven. Boeing avoided this danger by careful design of the wing and tail, and also by fitting a stall-warning system to prevent the stall occurring.

The other unique feature of the 727 was the first installation of an auxiliary power unit (APU) for starting and air conditioning. This, together with an integral access stair at the rear between the engines, meant the 727 was almost totally independent of ground facilities at the airports it used.

PRODUCTION AND INTO SERVICE

The magic 100 orders were achieved late in 1960 with 40 from Eastern Airlines together with 40 from United Airlines, who also negotiated an option to buy another 20. The 727 would be built.

Just two years later on November 27, 1962, the first aircraft, coded E-1 for Eastern (unlike with the 707, there was no prototype), was rolled out of the Renton factory, where it had been built alongside the 707. From the first flight in February 1963, the 727 had a reputation of being a pilot's plane, being easy to fly. It set the standard of handling for all airliners that followed it.

The first 727 was handed over to United Airlines on October 29, 1963, and both Eastern and United started regular services in February 1964. The first 727 was retired by United on January 13, 1991 after flying 64,500 hours and making 48,000 landings. It is now part of the Museum of Flight in Seattle.

The early 727 aircraft could carry a maximum of 131 passengers on the power of their three 14,000-pound-thrust Pratt & Whitney JT8D engines. However, in July 1967 the stretched 727-200 first flew with the fuselage lengthened by 20 feet. This particular version of the aircraft, with more powerful engines giving 16,000 pounds' thrust, could carry up to 189 passengers at a cruising speed of 599 m.p.h. Its range with a typical load was 2,800 miles.

Over a production life of 22 years, the 727 became the world's best-selling jet transport, the last of 1,831 being delivered in September 1984. Just as the 727 exceeded the production of the 707, the 737 in its turn has outsold the 727, as we shall see.

The last 15 727s to be sold were built purely as freighters with no provision for seats or windows. The customer buying these aircraft, Federal Express, was already operating a fleet of more than 50 used 727s converted to freighters. Today the majority of the 900 that are still in service are carrying cargo, not passengers.

With airliners continuing to fly for much longer than was originally envisaged when they were first produced, a number of programs have been initiated in order to monitor and assess these aging machines. The first aging aircraft maintenance program in the world was undertaken on a Boeing 727 aircraft in 1992, by the Marshall Aerospace Company of Cambridge, England.

ABOVE The seventh 727 for the launch customer, United Airlines, heads a mixed line up of new 707 and 727 airliners at Renton airfield.

LEFT With its tailplane and other substantial components removed, a Boeing 727 undergoes a major overhaul at Marshall Aerospace, England.

MODEL 737

The Boeing "baby" airliner was an unwanted child. Very nearly stillborn, when it did arrive, it was late and it was ugly! However, the ugly duckling grew up to be a swan—still not a beauty, except perhaps to the 4.3 billion passengers who have flown in the 737!

At the time of the 737's conception, Boeing designers were fully committed to other, more exciting programs like the stretched 727, the supersonic airliner, and what was to become the 747. There obviously was a market for a small jet liner carrying around 100 passengers, since Boeing had two existing

competitors. Douglas with the DC-9 and the British Aircraft Corporation with their BAC One-Eleven had together sold over 300 aircraft when the 737 was announced in February 1965. The unknown factor was how big the market was and whether it would stand another competitor, especially one two years behind its rivals. This was the 707-versus-DC-8 situation over again but with the Boeing now having to try to catch up.

THE DESIGN

The design, 21 examples of which Boeing had sold to their launch customer Deutsche Lufthansa, looked very different from

LEFT **The prototype Boeing 737, which first flew on April 9, 1967, during part of its flight test development program.**

BELOW **With their headquarters at Casablanca Airport, Morocco, Royal Air Maroc was founded in 1953 and currently operate thirteen 737s with a further ten on order.**

its 727 predecessor and from the Douglas and BAC jets. Boeing had deserted the tail-mounted engine configuration to return to engines mounted on the wing. However, unlike those of the 707, the engines were too near the ground to be hung from elegant struts but had to be slung directly under the wing.

However, it was the fuselage that gave the 737 its "Fluf" (Fat Little Ugly Fella) nickname. The aircraft had the same fuselage width as the 707 and 727, giving substantial manufacturing

savings and also creating an interior that felt like a much bigger airliner. The 737 had six-abreast seating; both the DC-9 and One-Eleven, with narrower cabins, had five-abreast seats. Passengers were to like the big jet atmosphere of the 737 even if it didn't look as pretty from the outside.

PRODUCTION

The 737-100 version ordered by Lufthansa was to be sold to only four customers, a total of 30 aircraft. It was an enlarged version, the 737-200, which United Airlines bought in April 1965, which put the 737 on the road to becoming an overwhelming success. Carrying up to 124 passengers, the 737-200 could fly 2,880 miles and land at remote airfields lacking much ground support equipment. Small airports worldwide could now have a jet service.

BELOW When compared with the earlier 737 above, the much greater diameter of the CFM56 turbofan engines and the characteristic flattened bottom lip of the engine cowlings is very apparent.

From the first 737-100 delivery to Lufthansa in December 1967 to the last 737-200 delivery in August 1988, 1,144 737s were manufactured. An impressive total, but the next model, the 737-300, with new and very fuel-efficient engines, introduced a family of jet airliners that have now pushed the total 737 sales past 4,000. The ugly duckling has truly become a swan!

THE 737 FAMILY

Boeing now offer a complete family of 737 "swans," all powered by versions of the CFM56 turbofan engines (the CFM56 is produced by CFMI, a joint venture by SNECMA of France and General Electric of the USA). The family ranges from the smallest, the 737-500, seating 110 passengers to the 737-900, capable of carrying up to 189 passengers. (The 737-600, -700, -800, and -900 are all termed next-generation models and feature a bigger wing, longer range, and a higher speed.)

Prices for 1998 vary from $38.5 million for the 737-300 to $85 million for the 737-900 version. The successful Boeing philosophy of giving the customer exactly the right size of airplane is typified by the 737. This philosophy was, however, started with the 707, when it was said that Boeing had a secret GFM (Great Fuselage Machine), which produced a continuous fuselage from which lengths were cut to suit airline requirements!

BOEING BUSINESS JET

The most recent variant to emerge from the Boeing fuselage sausage machine is the BBJ (Boeing Business Jet). A derivative of the 737-700, it first flew on September 4, 1998 and is aimed, as the name suggests, at the executive jet market. With a cabin of no less than 807 square feet, three times that of most of its competitors, plus a range of almost 7,000 miles, at a price of $34.25 million plus the cost of interior to suit, orders for 46 had been received by the end of 1998.

The outstanding success of the 737 concept and Boeing's ability to regularly update and improve it has meant that in 1998, 31 years after the first 737 flew, new orders appear almost daily to swell the 4,000-plus total order book. Of that number more than 2,700 are already in service with over 250 customer airlines in 95 countries. The best-selling commercial jetliner of all time has carried some 4.3 billion passengers—the equivalent of more than half the world's population.

At any one time over 700 Boeing 737s are in the air worldwide, carrying passengers. The competitors of 30 years ago are no more. The One-Eleven sales reached just 230; the DC-9 became the McDonnell Douglas MD 80/90 series and has sold well (1,000 plus). But in 1997 came the ultimate irony.

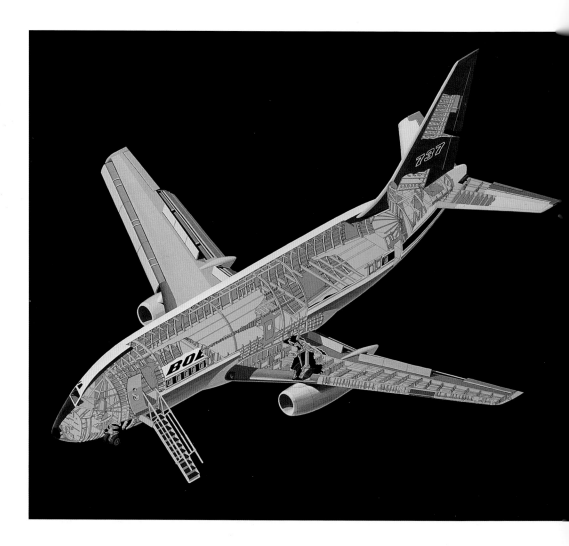

McDonnell Douglas was taken over by Boeing, who have now relaunched the MD 95 as their smallest product, the 100-seat Boeing Model 717-200. The first aircraft made its inaugural flight, shown live on the Internet, on September 2, 1998.

LEFT The family of Next Generation Boeing 737s display the range of fuselage lengths in this composite photograph.

LEFT ABOVE The construction details of the first 737 are revealed in this cut-away drawing.

LEFT BELOW One of South-West's fleet of 258 Boeing 737s transporting a full load of eager gamblers to Las Vegas.

RIGHT Based on the 737-700, orders for the Boeing Business Jet have boosted total 737 orders to well over 4,000 since 1967.

CHAPTER SEVEN

MODELS 747 TO 777

LEFT The power of its two Rolls-Royce RB.211 engines launches an American Airlines 757-200 into the air.

ABOVE Its passengers having spent all their dollars, a United Airlines Boeing 767 departs from Las Vegas.

The airplane that more than any other was to create the worldwide market for air travel for all was destined to be born at the worst possible time for Boeing.

The 747 had more than its share of early problems, especially with its engines, and it was to bring mighty Boeing closer to financial disaster than ever before. If the 747 program was an incredible gamble, then launching two new airliners, the 757 and the 767, simultaneously would appear even more foolhardy. In practice it was not so. The last of the quartet, the Boeing 777, conceived first as a stretched 767, was to be the first airliner to be totally computer-designed, using three-dimensional technology. There was no need to build a mock-up 777: the aircraft was preassembled on the computer, eliminating the need to physically position components and assemblies.

MODEL 747, THE JUMBO JET

Announced in April 1966, the Model 747 was an incredible act of faith by Boeing and Pan Am, who had ordered 25. Having rejected stretched versions of their 707 aircraft to carry 250 passengers (as Douglas had with the new stretched DC-8), Boeing believed it was possible to make a quantum step forward: the 400-seat airliner.

Losing a bitterly fought competition with Lockheed to build the heavy-lift transport for the US Air Force (the Lockheed C-5 Galaxy) was the spur Boeing needed. One of the founders of the Pan Am airline, the legendary Juan T. Trippe, having already been the first to order earlier Boeings like the models 307, 314, 377, and 707, was prepared, yet again, to be the first to operate a new Boeing. Therefore the Boeing board of directors agreed to build not only the world's biggest airliner but also the biggest factory in which to build it. A target date was set for a first flight on December 17, 1968 (the 65th anniversary of the Wright brothers' achievement).

Boeing had given themselves just three years from December 1965, when Pan Am had signed the letter of intent—three years to find a site for a new plant, to build the world's largest industrial facility (all under one roof), and to design and build an airliner that still, even today, dwarfs all others.

While the new factory was being created from 700 acres of forest at Everett, 40 miles north of Seattle, the Model 747 design was being finalized. In parallel, more orders were being urgently sought, even as the size of the aircraft grew to meet the requirements of Pan American. The final design looked much like a scaled-up 707 but with a distinctively bulged upper

BELOW A small proportion of the thousands of spectators, workers, and guests who attended the roll-out ceremony of the first Boeing Model 747 on September 30, 1968.

LEFT In a part of the world's largest manufacturing facility under one roof at Everett, Boeing 747 Jumbos are built for airline customers worldwide.

forward fuselage, housing the flight deck. This feature arose from the requirement that the 747 should have a potential dual role as a freighter. The upper flight deck would permit a front-opening cargo door giving clear access to the main cabin. In the late 1960s, Pan Am and the other airlines that bought the 747 believed that, in the future, passengers would fly supersonic, with the 747 relegated to carrying freight.

The team who did the impossible in creating both the plane and the plant called themselves, with full justification, "the Incredibles." Their work was unveiled for the first time on September 30, 1968, when the first 747 rolled out of the new Everett plant. The unofficial December 1968 first-flight target was always just beyond reach, the 747 first taking to its true element, the air, on February 9, 1969.

INTO SERVICE AND INTO PROBLEMS

The 747, which entered service on January 21, 1970, was substantially larger than that conceived in 1965. Capable of carrying up to 490 passengers or 113 tons (125 metric tonnes) of cargo, it had outgrown the only engines that were ready to power it. Although Boeing had looked at the engines being offered by General Electric and Rolls-Royce, only the Pratt & Whitney JT9D, producing 43,000 pounds of thrust, was able to meet the very tight delivery timetable.

Unfortunately for both Boeing and Pan Am, it was ready just in time, but reliability was somewhat lacking! On its inaugural Pan Am flight from London, *Clipper Young America* with 336 passengers on board suffered an overheating engine before take-off which could not be corrected. The flight eventually took off seven hours late in a substitute 747! The problems got worse. At one time Pan Am had five 747s in their hangar, grounded with engine problems.

For Boeing it was even worse!

Early in 1970, there were nearly 30 complete 747 airframes parked at Everett with concrete blocks where the engines should be. All this was happening during what was to prove to be the biggest ever crisis to hit Boeing.

RIGHT **A massive area of high lift flaps extend from the wings of a Pan American 747-212 as it approaches to land at London's Heathrow Airport.**

SINKING INTO DEBT

In the late 1960s the company had five major aircraft programs in progress. The 707, the 727, the 737, the 747, and the Super Sonic Transport (SST). The number of employees rose ever higher, as manpower was thrown at innumerable problems. But orders dried up as a worldwide recession, especially in air travel, began in 1969, continuing into 1970. Seventeen months went by, when not a single Boeing airliner was sold to a US airline. The final straw was the government cancelation, in March 1971, of the SST.

Boeing found itself more than $1 billion in debt.

The initial solution was to drastically reduce staff levels. From a high of 101,000 in 1968, by April 1971 Boeing's payroll in Seattle had shrunk to 38,000. No wonder that billboard appeared in the area reading: WILL THE LAST PERSON LEAVING SEATTLE TURN OUT THE LIGHTS (see Chapter One).

As well as laying off staff, Boeing sold off parts of its history. The historic Plant One (the first Boeing factory) went to the Seattle Port Authority, although the original Boeing factory was recovered to go to the planned Museum of Flight.

RECOVERY

Finally the company came through its financial problems and the 747-100 became an incredibly reliable airliner. One operated by Braniff International was, over a two-year period, flying an average of 14 hours every day (420 hours per month). Even this achievement has been overshadowed by more recent 747s, which have been flying 500 hours per month.

A special version of the Model 747-100 aircraft was developed. The 747SP (Special Performance) was 48 feet shorter, had the option of Rolls-Royce or General Electric engines, and was capable of carrying 300 passengers for over 7,600 miles. It seemed incredible at the time but regular, nonstop, services between New York and Tokyo became a fact in April 1976.

The next major 747 variant was the -300, which had an extension of the upper deck to accommodate up to 91 passengers. With the lower cabin capacity also increased by seven seats, the -300 could carry an incredible 630 passengers. Again airline customers could choose their engines from one of the big three manufacturers, P&W, GE, and R-R.

LEFT **The flight deck of an early 747-100 or a 747SP.**

BELOW LEFT **The 747SP (Special Performance) was derived from the 747-100 with a shorter fuselage to give a then incredible non-stop range of nearly 8,000 miles.**

RIGHT **The largest airliner carries the biggest spacecraft. A former American Airlines 747 was converted by Boeing in 1976/7 to the 747SCA (Shuttle Carrier Aircraft). Although trials proved that the Shuttle could be launched from the 747, the purpose of the SCA was to transport the Shuttle across the USA.**

RIGHT **A British Airways 747-400 is prepared for service in the large hangar of Marshall Aerospace, Cambridge.**

BELOW **In a special aboriginal livery, this Qantas 747 is one of the most colorful airliners in service.**

Externally the only visual change to distinguish the 747-400 from its 300 series predecessor were the six-foot-high "winglets" installed at the tips of the wings. However, this new model was such a revolutionary improvement on the earlier version that, within two years of its first flight in October 1998, sales of previous models ceased. The cockpit, for the first time, featured the Electronic Flight Instrument System (EFIS), the so-called "glass cockpit," in which large multifunction television screens display the information previously shown on conventional instruments. Now, more efficient versions of the Rolls-Royce RB-211, the Pratt & Whitney JT9D, and the General Electric CF6 enabled the maximum range to exceed 8,300 miles when carrying 416 passengers in three classes.

The 747-400 is currently offered in four versions: the standard passenger variant; the Domestic, able to carry 568 passengers over 2,075-mile stages; the Combi, giving the option of 410 passengers or 266 passengers and seven main-deck cargo pallets; and the Freighter, able to carry nearly 285,000 pounds of payload for over 5,000 miles. All the passenger versions have lower-hold cargo space of 6,000 cubic feet. Depending on the model you require, a new 1998 747-400 will cost you between $158.5 and $176.5 million.

Even before the -400 freighter, earlier versions of the 747 were fulfilling the cargo potential built into the design from the outset, either built as new Combi versions or converted from the earliest 747s. But it was the choice of the 747 for military and VIP functions that placed the highest seal of approval on the Boeing airliner.

ABOVE The setting sun glints on the underside of a Boeing 747 as it climbs away from the runway.

LEFT A 747-400 in the superseded British Airways livery on final approach to land at Heathrow Airport, London.

BELOW LEFT The potential for use as a freighter was built into the design from the start. Many of the earliest 747s are now converted for cargo, others are built specifically for that role.

AIR FORCE ONE

As with its 707 predecessor, the 747 was chosen to be the presidential aircraft. Two 747-200B variants, with air force designation C-25A, were modified and delivered to the US Air Force in 1990, replacing the 707s that had served seven presidents since 1962. Like its predecessors, the 747 is used not only by the President—when it uses radio call sign "Air Force One"— but also by other government personnel. Carrying up to 70 passengers with a crew of 23, the presidential 747s can be air-to-air refueled, giving virtually unlimited range.

Also capable of being refueled in flight is the E-4B version of the 747. Four of these highly specialized aircraft provide a National Airborne Operations Center able to coordinate the US national response to any emergency up to nuclear war. One E-4B aircraft is permanently on alert with its crew of up to 114. As with Air Force One, the electrical wiring throughout the aircraft is shielded to protect it from the effects of electromagnetic pulse (emp)—this is generated by a thermonuclear blast and is capable of causing severe damage to electrical and electronic equipment.

BELOW The presidential aerial carriage and presidents mountain. The latest "Air Force One" flies past the portraits of earlier presidents on Mount Rushmore.

To the end of October 1998, a total of 1,288 747s had been ordered, making it the third most popular Boeing airliner after the 737 and 727. With a recession, especially in the Far East, affecting new orders, deliveries during 1998 fell to just 10 from the 37 delivered in 1997. Consequently, planned production rates in 1999 have been reduced from 5 to 3.5 per month. However, with no viable replacement yet announced, who can say that the 747 will not exceed the 1,831 total of 727s built?

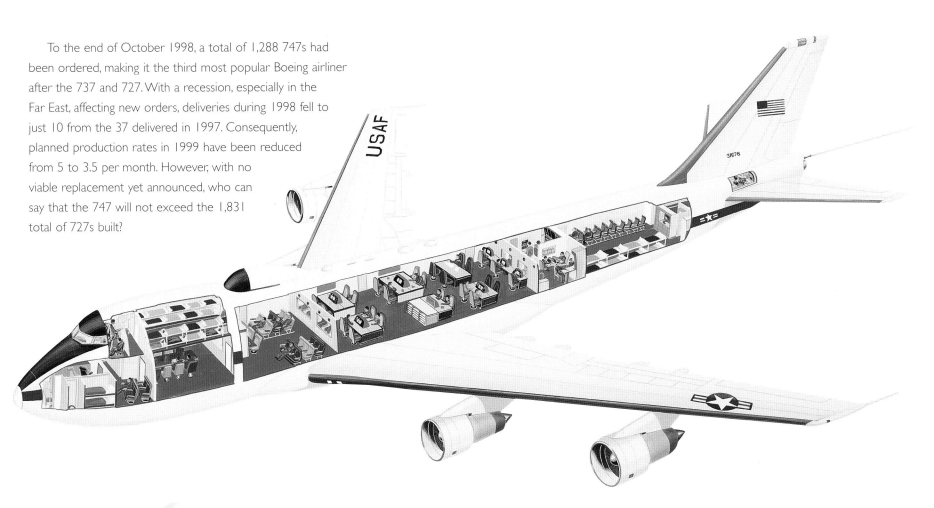

ABOVE This cut-away of the Boeing E-4B airborne command post shows the numerous communications suites, rest areas, and other facilities for the crew of up to 114.

RIGHT Of the four E-4B aircraft in the USAF inventory, one is always airborne to ensure that instant communications are available to the president in any sort of emergency.

MODELS 757 AND 767

The two aircraft that became models 757 and 767, with a high degree of commonality, started as two very different projects. The first mention of the 7X7, which was to become the 767, was in the company's 1972 annual report. Its sister was, for some time, referred to as the 7N7.

Even in the depths of the financial crises of the 1970s Boeing's designers were looking to the future.

The 7X7 was initially conceived as a STOL (Short Take-Off and Landing) aircraft for very short runways. The market for a STOL airliner was very limited. The 7X7 therefore evolved into a twin-engined wide-body airliner smaller than the tri-jet DC-10 and Tristar, but with much better economies.

The 7N7 started as a 727 replacement, again using a pair of the new, fuel-thrifty, big-fan engines, which were also much quieter than the early jets. In the fuel crises of the mid-1970s, when jet fuel in the USA went from 12 cents per gallon in 1973 to $1.1 a gallon in 1974, fuel economy was an imperative.

During the 1970s the two designs gradually came together until the 7N7/757 was the narrow-body version (same width as the 707-737 family), with the 7X7/767 as the wide-body version. Both had the same type of flight deck and systems, such that a pilot qualified on one could fly the other without additional training. This was to prove very attractive to airlines wishing to operate both aircraft: the 767, with its two aisles carrying around 230 passengers on the longer flights, and the single-aisle 757, with 180 passengers on the shorter services.

ROLL-OUTS

The 767 was the first to be unveiled in the now traditional Boeing roll-out. In front of 15,000 staff and guests the gleaming new model emerged into the sunshine of August 4, 1981. Built at an enlarged Everett plant, the 767 was scheduled to first join

United Airlines who, as the launch customer, had 30 aircraft on order. However, the success of the 767 was already assured by the time of the roll-out, as orders for 173 had been secured.

A little over five months later, on January 13, 1982, the slim, very fuel-efficient 757 had its day, this time at the Renton plant. Initially, orders for the 757 were slower to come than for its bigger sister. The launch customers of Eastern Airlines and British Airways had a total of 40 on order and were joined before the roll-out by Delta Air Lines, with a massive, record-breaking $3 billion order for 60 aircraft.

FIRST FLIGHTS, AND INTO SERVICE

The 767 flew first in September 1981 with the 757 following in February 1982. Whereas the 757 customers had initially a choice between Pratt & Whitney and Rolls-Royce engines, the 767 offered the Pratt & Whitney JT9 or the General Electric CF6. United Airlines put their first 767s into service with the Pratt & Whitney powerplant but the remaining 767 customers were evenly divided in their preference. This was not the case on the 757. Both launch airlines chose the Rolls-Royce RB211-535, and the RB211 has been the overwhelming first choice ever since.

ABOVE With a military designation of C-32A, four 757s were sold to the USAF to replace the last VIP 707s.

RIGHT Eastern Airlines, one of the two launch customers, were the first airline to receive the 757. Delivery was made in December 1982 and the first service was flown on January 1, 1983.

DEVELOPMENT

In common with all Boeing jetliners, both the 757 and 767 have been developed to meet the needs of the company's customer airlines. The 767 is now available in no fewer than six versions, the original -200 with its -200ER extended-range variant, the -300 has a fuselage 21 feet longer and is offered in standard, ER, and freighter models.

The latest 767-400ER is scheduled to be rolled out in August 1999 for delivery into service in May 2000. Intended to replace the first generation of European Airbuses as well as the Douglas DC-10 and Lockheed Tristar tri-jets, it is the first new aircraft to be jointly designed by Boeing's Commercial Airplane Group and the Douglas Products Division (formerly McDonnell Douglas). The -400 has a larger wing than the -300 and the 21-foot-longer fuselage increases the passenger capacity in the three classes to 245.

Similarly, the 757-300, which was rolled out in May 1998, is 23 feet longer than its -200 predecessor and can carry 20 percent more passengers—up to 289 in full tourist class. At nearly 179 feet long, it is the longest single-aisle twin-jet Boeing has ever made (with the same fuselage width, the longest 707 was just 153 feet). For the first time ever, the inaugural flight of a new aircraft was watched live on the Internet. Computer users who linked to the Boeing website on August 2, 1998 watched the first 757-300 take to the air. With its Rolls-Royce engines, the -300 is expected to be delivered to the German launch customer Condor Flugdienst in January 1999.

Both of the Boeing twins have produced very specialized military versions, especially the 767.

RIGHT With smoke trailing from its tires, the first 767-300ER lands after a test flight.

TOP In 1998, Delta Airlines operated a fleet of 91 Pratt & Whitney powered Boeing 757s, two of which are seen here at Phoenix, Arizona.

ABOVE On final approach to Las Vegas, with landing gear and all flaps down, is a United Airlines 767-300.

THE MILITARY TWINS

Seeking to produce a replacement for its famous KC-135 and the other military variants of the 707, including the E-3 AWACS, Boeing are promoting the 767 as that replacement. To date, the only success has been the sale of four 767 AWACS to the Japan Air Self-Defense Force, where they are designated E-767. It is fitted with the standard 30-foot-diameter rotating radome of the E-3, and its two General Electric CF-6 turbofans can give a patrol time of 13 hours at a range of 300 miles from base. A crew of up to 21 are carried.

The 757 military success has been the sale and delivery of four planes—designated C-32A—to the US Air Force as a replacement for the last of the VC-137 VIP versions of the 707 plane. As with all VIP aircraft, including the two 747 Air Force One planes, the C-32s will be based at Andrews Air Force Base, Maryland.

BOEING AND ROLLS-ROYCE

The growing acceptance of Rolls-Royce engines with Boeing's customer airlines can be best judged by the fact that a Rolls-Royce option is available for the majority of Boeing commercial aircraft.

Rolls-Royce first put a jet engine onto a Boeing jet in the mid 1950s. The installation of the Conway made the 1956 sale of the 707-400 to BOAC, the British national carrier, slightly more palatable to the UK public. The next Boeing use of Rolls-Royce engines was more than 20 years later when the RB-211 became an option for the 747.

The RB-211 was the engine that in the mid-1960s Rolls-Royce had sold to Lockheed to power its L-1011 Tristar in the face of fierce competition from General Electric. It was also the engine whose development costs were to force Rolls-Royce into bankruptcy in February 1971.

After a period of nationalization the private company re-emerged to develop the RB-211 into a range of commercial turbofans, giving a combination of reliability and economy unsurpassed elsewhere. They are also among the quietest and most environmentally friendly engines in their class. That is why the RB-211 is the first choice for the 757, why it was fitted to the 2,000th wide-body airliner (a 747-400) to emerge from Everett, and why the Trent 800 version will be fitted to over 40 percent of the 428 Boeing 777s on order at the time of writing.

Rolls-Royce engines have also been chosen to re-equip the Boeing 727 freighters of United Parcel Service, and BMW Rolls-Royce engines are fitted to the Boeing 717 aircraft.

ORDERS AND DELIVERIES

At the end of October 1998, of the 942 757s on order, 823 had been delivered to their customers; the figures for the 767 are 848 on order and 720 delivered. Boeing's bold decision to launch two new aircraft virtually together has had the financial success it deserved.

ABOVE The United Arab Emirates airline is based in Dubai but has worldwide services. In addition to the Boeing 777 seen here, Emirates also operates a fleet of Airbus A300 and A310.

LEFT Boeing have chosen the 767 airframe to be the successor to the 707 based E-3 Sentry. At the time of printing, Japan was the first and only customer for the 767 AWACS.

THE MODEL 777

The latest Boeing and, in its -300 version, the longest airliner in the world, first flew in 1994. Designed to fill the size gap between the 767 and the 747, the first -200 aircraft could seat up to 320 passengers in three classes and was delivered to United Airlines in May 1995.

COMPUTER-DESIGNED

The world's first jet airliner to be designed wholly on the computer, including solid-image pre-assembly of all the components and fittings, the 777 had no need of an expensive, full-scale physical mock-up. The scale of this is hard to comprehend. The Seattle area had no fewer than 1,700 individual computer workstations linked to four IBM mainframe computers. These were further linked to mainframes and other workstations in Philadelphia, Wichita, and even Japan. Not a drawing board or slide rule in sight!

VARIANTS

In addition to the standard -200 model, a long-range (up to 8,860 miles) -200ER version is available. The 777-300, with its fuselage stretched by 33 feet to 242 feet 4 inches, can carry as many as 550 passengers in an all-economy configuration. With a range of nearly 6,500 miles—say, San Francisco to Tokyo—the 777-300 is comparable to the early 747 aircraft but has 40 percent lower maintenance costs and burns one-third less fuel.

A new 777-300 costs between $151 million and $173.5 million, much the same as a 747-400. The first -300 with Rolls-

Royce engines was handed over to its launch customer, Cathay Pacific, in May 1998.

Of the 428 777s on order by the end of October 1998, 163 had been delivered with production rates steady at 25 a year. The 777 is therefore scheduled to be built until at least 2008, even if no more are ordered, which is highly unlikely, especially as a 10,000-mile-range variant of the -200 is currently being planned.

LEFT United Airlines were the first to put the new 777-200 into service in 1995. Here one of their aircraft in the new company livery was photographed at London Heathrow in 1998.

BELOW With two giant Rolls-Royce Trent turbofan engines, Cathay Pacific Airways of Hong Kong were, in 1998, the first to put the 777-300 into service.

CHAPTER EIGHT

FROM ROTARY TO SUPERSONIC

LEFT Escorted by an F-16 chase plane, the F-22 Raptor carries out slow speed handling tests with its landing gear down.

ABOVE The unveiling of the B-2, the USA's most secret and expensive bomber, in November 1989, gave little idea of its shape and capabilities.

Boeing entered the helicopter market in 1960 when it acquired the Vertol Aircraft Corporation. The financial reasons for the acquisition were obvious. Vertol, formerly the Piasecki Helicopter Corporation (after its founder, Frank Piasecki) had substantial orders from the United States Navy and Army for a version of its company-funded Model 107 prototype.

But Vertol were in Philadelphia, nearly 2,400 miles from Seattle. The workforce were fiercely loyal to their founder. The new managers brought in to solve severe production problems were bitterly resented—a formula for bad industrial relations, which were to plague the Vertol Division (later Boeing Helicopters) for almost two decades. However, during that time and since, many superb helicopters were built.

THE BOEING VERTOL MODEL 107 AND CH-46 SEA KNIGHT

Based on the success of their Piasecki HUP-1—the "Flying Banana," the Model 107, powered by two Lycoming shaft turbines, first flew in August 1958. The US Army had already ordered 10, later reduced to three in favor of an enlarged Model 114. Meanwhile the US Navy had chosen the Vertol

107M as its future medium-lift transport helicopter with an initial order for 50, the first flying in1962.

Designed to carry a 4,000-pound load or 17 fully equipped troops at a speed of 150 m.p.h. over a combat radius of 115 miles, the Sea Knight was an immediate success. A final total of 666 Model 107s had been built and delivered to the US Navy, Marines, and other users when US production of the aircraft ceased in 1971.

Powered by two General Electric T58 turboshaft engines giving a maximum of 1,870 shaft horsepower (shp), the aircraft has had regular upgrades and improvements throughout its service life. Boeing is supplying the navy with 421 kits to replace the rotary parts of the engine/rotor mechanisms under a $375 million contract scheduled to be completed in 2000.

In addition to the US production, the Model 107 has been built, under license in Japan, by Kawasaki Heavy Industries. Fabrication of 160 examples started in 1961 and was completed in February 1990.

Other users of the Model 107 from both US and Japanese production have been New York Airways, the Canadian Air Force, the Swedish Navy, and Saudi Arabia.

BELOW **A CH-46 Sea Knight demonstrates its controllability by hovering with its rear wheels on a rocky outcrop.**

TOP RIGHT **The original Vertol Model 107 shows its amphibious capabilities which led to large orders from the US Navy.**

RIGHT **The latest CH-47D Chinook in service with the US Army and many other air forces.**

THE BOEING VERTOL MODEL 114, THE CH-47 CHINOOK

Declared the winner of a design competition for a heavy-lift army helicopter in March 1959, the Model 114 was substantially larger than its Model 107 predecessor. It was capable of carrying up to 40 fully equipped troops or an internal 6,000-pound payload for a distance of 115 miles. An underslung external load of around six tons could also be carried for over 20 miles. This weight-lifting power came from two 2,200-shp Lycoming T55 turboshafts driving two 59-foot-diameter intermeshing rotors. Interlinking between the two rotor heads prevents the two rotors coming into contact and enables either or both engines to provide the power.

After ground tests in spring 1961, the Chinook flew for the first time in September of that year. After entering service with the US Army, the CH-47A soon became the undisputed Vietnam war partner of the Bell UH-1 "Huey." Repeat orders followed rapidly and, at the peak, 29 Chinooks a month were rolling off the Vertol production lines.

THE CH-47D

With steadily increasing power from its engines, improved variants of the CH-47 continued to be produced and appeared until the present D model, which can carry a useful load of 25,000 pounds. The current Textron Lycoming T55-L engines are more than twice as powerful as those engines originally fitted to the A model, giving a maximum output of nearly 4,900 shp.

More than 800 Chinook aircraft have been built, of which some 600 are still in service, both in the USA and elsewhere in the world. Most of the earlier versions are being brought up to CH-47D standards. With no viable replacement, the Chinook remains in production for the United States and overseas military forces. The US Army expect to operate the Chinook well beyond 2020.

CIVIL AND SPECIAL CHINOOKS

Under the model number 234, a civil version of the CH-47D was introduced in 1978 for use by offshore oil-exploration companies and other prospecting duties in remote areas. With 44 seats in the airliner-type interior, it attracted its first commercial order for six aircraft from British Airways Helicopters for offshore use over the North Sea

The MH-47E is the Special Operations Chinook, designed to perform covert operations over a 350-mile radius in almost any weather, day or night. The MH-43E has the most advanced communications and navigational equipment ever fitted to an army helicopter. Fitted with infrared and advanced radar, the Chinook can fly at near-zero feet in conditions that would ground most helicopters. Delivery of the E model was completed in 1995.

THE CHINOOK IN COMBAT—VIETNAM, THE FALKLANDS, AND THE GULF

The Chinook has been proven in combat in at least three different wars. Vietnam was the conflict that made the helicopter an indispensable part of modern warfare. First used in 1965, within three years the Chinook had flown over 160,000 hours carrying nearly 22,500,000 passengers and over 1.4 million tons of cargo. Underslung loads ranged from 105 mm howitzer guns to damaged aircraft. Frequently the loads, carried both externally and internally, far exceeded the officially permitted maxima. During the last frenetic days of the war, one Chinook was recorded as carrying 147 refugees in a single journey.

Britain sent four RAF Chinook HC-1 helicopters to the 1982 Falklands War. Carried on the converted civilian cargo ship *Atlantic Conveyor*, the precious load arrived in the vicinity of the Falklands on May 25, 1982. The first Chinook had been reassembled and flown off by late afternoon when the ship was hit by two Exocet missiles and quickly sank. The sole surviving Chinook, with its code letters BN, was Britain's only heavy-lift helicopter for the rest of the conflict and was worked very hard. During the initial attack on Goose Green, 81 fully armed paratroops were crammed into Bravo November—there wasn't room for any more.

At the start of the ground war during Operation Desert Storm in the 1991 Gulf War, Chinooks of the US Army and the Coalition air forces helped carry the XVIII Corps in a 250-mile flanking movement to encircle the Iraqi forces. The airborne elements of the XVIII Corps included units of the American 82nd and 101st Airborne Divisions, whose predecessors had parachuted into Normandy in June 1944. Modern troops used the mighty Chinook.

BELOW The Chinook (this is an RAF aircraft) has a very characteristic sound in the air caused by the interaction of its twin rotors, once heard, never forgotten.

THE AH-64 APACHE

When, in 1997, Boeing merged with McDonnell Douglas, the
virtual takeover meant Boeing acquired some of the world's
most potent aircraft. None is more potent than the latest AH-
64D Apache Longbow battlefield attack helicopter. The AH-64D
being built in Mesa, Arizona, is the current production version of
the Apache, which is in service around the world with the US
Army and the forces of Greece, Israel, Kuwait, Saudi Arabia, and
the United Arab Emirates. More than 900 of the AH-64A
version were built.

Fitted with the Longbow fire-control radar, the two-seat
Apache can detect, identify, and attack stationary and moving
targets with a range of missiles and gun armament. Production
of the D model is continuing at more than three aircraft a
month with deliveries to the US Army and the Royal
Netherlands Air Force. The first Apache for the British Army
flew in May 1998, powered by two Rolls-Royce/Turbomeca RTM
322 turboshafts. The UK Army Air Corps has 67 Apache
Longbows on order, to be license-built by GKN Westland in the
UK. First deliveries are expected from March 2000.

COLLABORATIVE PROJECTS

As aircraft become ever more complex, especially military types, these are increasingly being designed and built as collaborative projects. Despite being the largest aerospace company in the world, Boeing has found advantage in participating in a number of these projects. In fact, in the future, it is most unlikely that any advanced aircraft system will be designed and produced by a single aerospace company.

THE BOEING-SIKORSKY RAH-66 COMANCHE

A future battlefield partner to Boeing's Apache attack helicopter, the Comanche, will be the US Army's armed reconnaissance helicopter from 2006—the world's first "stealthy" helicopter, with features to make it difficult to detect by both radar and thermal (infrared) methods. Able to fly faster and outmaneuver all other combat helicopters currently in production, the RAH-66 is a twin-turbine, two-seat, light attack-and-reconnaissance helicopter.

To ensure its "stealthy" appearance is not compromised in any way, the fixed armament of a three-barrel 20 mm Gatling gun can be neatly and safely stowed away, and the missile armament is also fully retractable. The armament will be fired by the same Longbow fire-control system as fitted to the Apache Longbow.

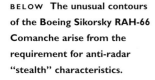

BELOW The unusual contours of the Boeing Sikorsky RAH-66 Comanche arise from the requirement for anti-radar "stealth" characteristics.

The RAH-66 development contract was awarded in 1991 to "Team Comanche," led by Boeing Helicopters, Philadelphia, and the United Technologies' Sikorsky Aircraft of Stratford, Connecticut. The other member companies of the team include Boeing Electronic Systems of Seattle, General Dynamics, Hamilton Standard, Lockheed Martin, and Northrop Grumman—in fact most of the leading companies in US aerospace.

The first Comanche flew in January 1996 from Sikorsky's development flight test center in West Palm Beach, Florida. After what was called "a comprehensive inspection and installation of various system improvements" the prototype took to the air again in October 1998. It is expected to be joined by the second prototype aircraft in March 1999.

THE BELL-BOEING V-22 OSPREY

The helicopter's ability to take off vertically has always incurred a penalty: a much slower top speed than that of conventional fixed-wing aircraft. Two hundred m.p.h. is fast for a helicopter! Since the 1950s a number of research aircraft have been built attempting to combine the helicopter's ability to take off vertically with the 300–400 m.p.h. top speed of a propeller aircraft. None were truly successful, although Bell had flown the XV-3 tilt-rotor craft in 1958. The later Bell XV-15, although still an experimental aircraft, reached 350 m.p.h. and was the star of the 1981 Paris Air Salon.

LEFT The "stealthy" shape of the Comanche is very apparent in this close-up photograph of the tail, taken during the 1998 Farnborough Airshow in England.

BELOW Not looking at all like helicopters, a pair of V-22 Ospreys show why the US Marines are very keen to receive their high-speed, vertical take-off transports as soon as possible.

It was in 1983 that Boeing Helicopters and Bell Helicopter Textron won a design contract for a twin-engined tilt-rotor aircraft based on the XV-15 concept. With its two turboprop engines mounted at the wing tips, able to rotate from vertical to horizontal, the aircraft would take off vertically, before translating into horizontal flight and vice versa. Boeing assumed responsibility for the fuselage, digital avionics, and flight controls with Bell building the wing, tail, rotor systems, and engine installation.

The V-22 is designed to carry 24 troops or 20,000 pounds of cargo internally or underslung. Its rotors are cross-coupled so that either Allison T406 engine can power the rotors in the event of an engine failure. A top speed of over 390 m.p.h. is possible from the two 6,150-shp engines.

The first Osprey flew in March 1989, followed in succession by the rest of the six development aircraft. The fifth crashed in June 1991 owing to an avionics mis-wiring, fortunately without a fatality. The test program has been somewhat protracted, as might be expected from such a revolutionary concept. Initial

estimates of entry into service in the early 1990s have passed by. However, the aircraft is now in production with the Marine Corps expecting to get the first of their required 425 aircraft during 1999–2000. The Special Operations Force want 50 and the navy have a requirement for 48 as an antisubmarine aircraft. For carrier operations the rotors fold and the wing rotates to facilitate storage.

With most of the technical problems resolved, the only outstanding problem is the cost. The early development aircraft cost nearly $42 million each. The final cost of the production example should be nearer $30 million, depending upon how many are finally ordered.

THE B-2A SPIRIT, THE "STEALTH BOMBER"

At the peak of the B-2 program, Boeing had 10,000 people employed on this project. Officially a Strategic Low Observable Penetration Bomber, the B-2 is without doubt the world's most advanced and most expensive bomber. The ending of the Cold

BELOW The view of the B-2 Spirit Stealth bomber that it was not possible to see at its roll-out in 1989. A unique tailless design which achieves its low radar signature by a very different technical solution than the earlier F-117 Stealth Fighter.

ABOVE **The first pre-production F-22 Raptor is one of nine airframes which will evaluate the complete F-22 weapon system before entry into service in 2005.**

War has meant that, instead of the original 133 aircraft, just 21 are being delivered, the first having entered service in December 1993. It is likely that each aircraft will have cost over $2.2 billion.

The B-2 team are led by the Northrop Grumman Corporation, at whose plant in Palmdale, California, the aircraft was assembled. Boeing's responsibility was the manufacture of parts of the fuselage, including the weapons bay and fuel tanks, as well as the fuel systems, weapons delivery system, and landing gear. Other major members of the team are Vought, Hughes, CAE-Link, and General Electric, plus some 4,000 subcontractors. Boeing has completed its part of the current order, but the team continues to provide product support and, if further orders were forthcoming, could re open production.

THE F-22 RAPTOR

During the 1980s the US Air Force evolved a requirement for an air-superiority fighter to replace the renowned F-15 Eagle. A formal request for a proposal was issued in September 1985 for what was then called the ATF (Advanced Tactical Fighter).

Lockheed, with Boeing and General Dynamics, offered the YF-22. The competing YF-23 was built by Northrop and McDonnell Douglas, and the first of two examples flew in August 1990. A month later the initial YF-22 also flew. After competitive evaluation by the air force, the Lockheed/Boeing/General Dynamics F-22 was declared the winner in April 1991.

A contract to build nine production F-22As, plus two ground test frames, was signed at a cost of $9.55 billion. It is termed an Engineering and Manufacturing Development (EMD) contract, and its value has since risen to $15 billion. A total future requirement for 648 aircraft was announced at that time.

The 1990s reorganization within the American aerospace industry has meant that Lockheed has become Lockheed Martin, which also incorporates part of General Dynamics and thus has 67.5 percent of the project. Boeing's 32.5 percent consists of the rear fuselage, wings, radar, power supplies, mission software, and life-support systems. The two Pratt & Whitney F119 engines give the Raptor a maximum speed in excess of Mach 2 (twice the speed of sound).

The single-seat F-22 is designed to be exceptionally maneuverable, its engines having vectoring exhaust nozzles to enhance that capability. The stealth technology will minimize the radar cross-section of the aircraft, which, with advanced long-range missiles, will make the Raptor the most potent fighter in the world.

Air Combat Command of the US Air Force is expecting to take delivery of its first aircraft in 2005 as the F-15 begins to be phased out. Current procurement plans are for 339 aircraft with production being completed by 2012. The total estimated cost of that program is $43.4 billion. When added to the EMD program, each F-22 will therefore have cost around $183 million or about six F-16 Fighting Falcons. For that sum the pilots of the twenty-first century will be flying what has been called the "ultimate fighter." It will certainly be the most expensive and sophisticated one.

THE JSF (JOINT STRIKE FIGHTER)

In the same way as two competing designs fought for the ATF (later F-22) contract, so in 2001, either Boeing or Lockheed Martin will be chosen to build the JSF.

Many times in the past, the aircraft industry has attempted to produce one design able to meet the often conflicting requirements of both the air force and the navy, usually without any real success.

The ATF is attempting to achieve what, at first sight, appears to be impossible.

The air force wants a conventional-take-off-and-landing strike aircraft to replace its present F-16 fighters and A-10 attack aircraft. The US Navy also needs a strike aircraft to perform the A-6 Intruder's role. The US Marine Corps wish to replace their conventional F/A-18 fighters and the AV-8B Harriers. However, the Harrier is a STOVL aircraft (Short Take-Off and Vertical Landing). Joining the Marines is the British Royal Navy, who would like a replacement aircraft for their aging Sea Harriers. A potential market for nearly 3,000 aircraft if Boeing can achieve a miracle.

Boeing has a very strong team in the JSF project, including Pratt & Whitney (makers of the thrust vectoring engines for the F-22) and Rolls-Royce (manufacturers of the Pegasus engine in the Harrier). Also from the UK are Flight Refuelling Limited, Dowty Aerospace, GEC-Marconi, Messier-Dowty, and Martin

Baker. Major US aerospace companies include Litton, Northrop Grumman, Honeywell, Allied Signal, Sundstrand, and Raytheon.

When the two prototypes of both competing designs fly toward the end of the year 2000, the Boeing design with its single Pratt & Whitney F119 engine (a pair of which are in the F-22) and its Rolls-Royce STOVL technology must be the strong favorite. If it does win it will be the first Boeing-led fighter since the P-26 Peashooter of the mid 1930s.

MODEL 2707

With that model number it must be the ultimate Boeing airliner for the year 2000 and beyond! Boeing's and the United States' supersonic-airliner answer to Concorde, maybe. Well, it might have been, but regrettably only a full-sized mock-up was ever designed and built.

THE SUPERSONIC TRANSPORT

Boeing's early research into a supersonic transport started in the 1950s but on a very small scale. It became a formal project under model number 733 in 1958 but it was soon obvious that the aircraft envisaged was beyond the resources of a single company. As Concorde's designers had chosen Mach 2.2 as its top speed, the Boeing SST had to go faster. The Anglo-French Concorde was built of aluminum alloys, which would be weakened by the excessive heat generated at speeds in excess of Mach 2.2—about 1,450 m.p.h. Therefore Boeing chose a titanium alloy for their aircraft that would be capable of Mach 2.7 (around 1,800 m.p.h.). Also, as Concorde was considered to be too small with its maximum of 140 passengers, the 733 would be able of carrying up to 227 passengers.

In 1963, the US government launched an SST (Super Sonic Transport) competition which was 90 percent government-funded. Boeing entered its Model 733, enlarged to carry 300 passengers and with a variable-sweep wing to give a landing speed and noise levels comparable with the first generation of jet liners.

The mock-up of this revolutionary aircraft cost $11 million to produce and was unveiled on September 29, 1966 under the official designation of Boeing 2707. Lockheed's equally expensive mock-up was a double delta, which had been revealed three months earlier.

The decision was announced on 31 December 1966: the Federal Aviation Agency had chosen Boeing!

Having won the competition, Boeing began to have second thoughts on the "swing wing." To Lockheed's disgust, the Model 2707 became a delta but with a horizontal tail. Approval to build two prototypes was gained in 1969 with a first flight scheduled for 1973, but a storm was brewing.

RIGHT Like its much smaller European counterpart, Concorde, the nose of the Boeing 2707 was designed to have a retractable visor and to droop for landing and take-off. What a sight that would have been!

GREEN ISSUES

For the first time ever, environmental issues were to have a decisive influence on a major aeronautical project. Noise was but one aspect of the public's concern in a massive anti-SST campaign, which was to rage on both sides of the Atlantic. It was said that supersonic flight would make passengers sterile, destroy the ozone layer, and worse! Concorde was to survive this attack, but only because the French refused to tear up the international agreement with Britain.

CANCELATION

The end for America's SST came on March 24, 1971 when Congress refused to vote further funds for the project. More than $1 billion had already been spent with an estimate that the total cost of the two prototypes would reach $4 billion. Had the public been behind the project, then even that cost would have been acceptable.

But nobody in the USA wanted a supersonic transport—not the airlines, who had massive commitments for wide-bodied airliners; not the public, who were afraid of the noise, the sonic bang, and all the other scare stories; perhaps not even Boeing, who, even if they were paying only 10 percent of the cost, could probably see that it would never make money.

The $11 million mock-up aircraft was sold for $31,000, completely dismantled, and shipped to Florida, where, with nearby Walt Disney World® it became a tourist attraction until it finally faded away in the early 1990s.

The Model 2707 is a "what might have been." Perhaps, as with Concorde, its economics and sales prospects would have been shattered by the fuel-price crisis of the mid-1970s when the cost of jet fuel increased tenfold. Or maybe, as always in the past, speed would have sold seats and it would have been the 747 Jumbo that became the White Elephant.

BELOW The artist's impression of the Boeing SST with its wings fully swept back, flying at 1,800 miles per hour at 64,000 feet.

BOTTOM The giant size of the Boeing SST can be judged by the figure in this photograph of the $11 million mock-up.

BIBLIOGRAPHY

Anderton, David A., 1975. *Strategic Air Command*. London. Ian Allan

Boeing Company. 1977. *Pedigree of Champions—Boeing Since 1916*.

Boeing Historical Archives. 1991. *Year by Year—75 Years of Boeing History 1916–1991.*

Boeing website: http://www.boeing.com

Bowers, Peter M. 1989. *Boeing Aircraft Since 1916*. London: Putnam.

Bowers, Peter M. *Profile No. 2: The Boeing P-12E*. Profile Publications: Windsor.

Bowers, Peter M. *Profile No. 14: The Boeing P-26A*. Profile Publications: Windsor.

Bowers, Peter M. 1965. *Profile No. 27: The Boeing F4B-4*. Profile Publications: Windsor.

Bowers, Peter M. 1966. *Profile No. 83: Boeing B-47*. Profile Publications: Windsor.

Bowers, Peter M. 1966. *Profile No. 97: The American DH4*. Profile Publications: Windsor.

Burden, Draper, Rough, Smith, and Wilton. 1986. *Falklands—The Air War*. London: Arms and Armour Press.

Coyne, James P. 1992. *Air Power in the Gulf*. Arlington, Virginia. Air Force Association.

Francillon, René J. 1988. *McDonnell Douglas Aircraft Since 1920*. London: Putnam.

Freeman, Roger A. 1970. *The Mighty Eighth—A History of the US 8th Army Air Force*. London: Macdonald and Company.

Freeman, Roger A. 1981. *Mighty Eighth War Diary*. London: Janes.

Frisbee, John L. 1987. *Makers of the United States Air Force*. Washington, DC: Office of the Air Force History.

Gunston, Bill. 1986. *World Encyclopaedia of Aero Engines*. London: Book Club Associates/Patrick Stephens Ltd.

Gurney, Gene (Colonel, USAF, retd.). 1985. *Vietnam—The War in the Air*. London: Sidgwick and Jackson.

Johnson, A.M. "Tex" (with Charles Barton). 1991. *"Tex" Johnson Jet-Age Test Pilot*. Washington, DC: Smithsonian Press.

Lambert, Mark. 1992. *Jane's All the World's Aircraft 1992–93*. London: Janes.

Lee, David. 1998. *World War II Aeroplanes*. London: Apple.

Longyard, William J. 1994. *Who's Who in Aviation History*. Shrewsbury: Airlife Publishing Ltd.

Mason, Francis K., and Windrow, Martin C. 1970. *Air Facts and Feats*. London: Guinness Superlatives.

Price, Alfred. 1967. *Profile No. 192: Boeing 707*. Profile Publications: Windsor.

Serling, Robert J. 1992. *Legend and Legacy—The Story of Boeing and its People*. New York: St Martin's Press.

Swanborough, F.G. 1963. *United States Military Aircraft Since 1909*. London: Putnam.

Swanborough, Gordon, and Bowers, Peter M. 1976. *United States Navy Aircraft Since 1911*. London: Putnam.

Taylor, John W.R. 1966. *Jane's All the World's Aircraft 1966–67*. London: Janes.

Thetford, Owen. 1979. *Aircraft of the Royal Air Force Since 1918*. London: Putnam.

Watson, George, Tsouras, and Cyr. 1991. *Military Lessons of the Gulf War*. London: Greenhill Books.

Journals include *Rolls-Royce World, Aircraft Illustrated, Air Classics,* and *Air Combat.*

ACKNOWLEDGMENTS

I wish to acknowledge, with gratitude, the encouragement and assistance of the following:

John Batchelor; Owen Dinsdale; John Gaertner of the EAA Museum; Bill Harrison; Terry Holloway of Marshall Aerospace; Mike Leister of the AMC Museum; Tom Lubbesmeyer of Boeing Archives; Ed Maloney of the Air Museum, Planes of Fame; Bob Mikesh, formerly of the National Air and Space Museum; Graham Simons of GMS Enterprises and the three people, without whom this book would not have been written: my editor, Clare Hubbard; Linda Mason, my former secretary at Duxford, England; and my beloved wife, Jeannie.

GENERAL INDEX

Picture Credits

MODEL INDEX